Windows 8 in the Enterprise

Andreas Stenhall

PUBLISHED BY
Deployment Artist
http://www.deploymentartist.com

Warning and Disclaimer

Feedback Information

We'd like to hear from you! If you have any comments about how we could improve the quality of this book, please don't hesitate to contact us by visiting www.deploymentfundamentals.com, sending an email to feedback@deploymentfundamentals.com, or visiting our Facebook site www.facebook.com/deploymentfundamentals.

Acknowledgements

Thanks goes out to my dear family, with Anna my wife showing patience as the writing of this book has taken quite some time. Without the support from my wife and kids, this book could never have been written.

I would also like to thank Johan Arwidmark at Deployment Artist for giving me the great opportunity to write this book. Without him, this book would never have been written.

About the Author

Andreas Stenhall is a Senior Technical Architect at Coligo, specializing in the Windows client in terms of deployment, management, and optimization for enterprises and governments. When not providing hands-on consulting services, Andreas lectures, leads workshops, and teaches courses on Windows client and server. He has spoken at various Microsoft conferences, including prominent TechEd events both in the US and in Europe.

Andreas is deeply involved in the community and has been awarded with the Microsoft Most Valuable Professional title as "Windows Expert ITPRO" every year since 2009. He also runs the Swedish-speaking community www.alltomwindows.se and an English-language blog for IT professionals, named "The Experience Blog" (www.theexperienceblog.com).

Andreas is certified as a Microsoft Certified Solutions Associate in Windows Server 2008 and Windows 7, along with a number of other related certifications in Windows client and server.

Contents

Contents

Introduction

Windows 8 in the Enterprise is the ultimate source for IT Pros who want to take full advantage of and implement Windows 8 in their enterprise.

Without doubt there are challenges bringing Windows 8 into an organization. But, at the same time, Windows 8 offers great possibilities and improvements that you can take advantage of. Windows 8 not only solves your most common on-premises problems, but also introduces new opportunities for your users to work efficiently and from anywhere, while keeping machines and data more secure than ever.

Unlike most other books on the topic "Windows client," the focus of this book is entirely enterprise environments and what is relevant in terms of managing, automating, and optimizing in these kinds of environments. The book is based on many years of experience with Windows deployments and management projects, and it contains a wealth of real-world tips and tricks that reflect how enterprises actually use Windows features.

Say Hello (Possibly Again) to ViaMonstra Inc.

In this book, you deploy and configure Windows 8 for the fictive ViaMonstra Inc. organization. ViaMonstra is a company with one primary location with 3000 employees in New York and with a small subsidiary in Stockholm.

ViaMonstra is running Windows XP in parallel with Windows 7.

The name ViaMonstra comes from *Viam Monstra*, Latin, meaning "Show me the way."

Structure of the Book

The first chapter covers the basic topics, such as architecture, editions, and features. It also describes how to deploy Windows 8 and deal with licensing and activation. Chapter 2 is dedicated to the brand new user interface in Windows 8, along with modern-style apps and the two faces of Internet Explorer.

Chapter 3 is about user data and profiles and deals with setting them up correctly. It also features an exceptionally useful new tool, User Experience Virtualization (UE-V). Chapter 4 deals with security in various aspects.

In Chapter 5, you learn about virtualization. Chapter 6 covers mobility scenarios and remote access.

Chapter 7 and 8 are all about management, troubleshooting, and recovery once you get Windows 8 deployed in your enterprise environment.

Chapter 9 is about adding value to the Windows client using the Microsoft Desktop Optimization Pack and the tools that are included in it.

Finally, you have the appendix, which includes extra material on how to set up the lab environment, server and client, including their roles and configurations.

How to Use This Book

The book is packed with step-by-step guides, which mean you will be able to build your deployment solution as you read along.

In numbered steps, all names and paths are set in bold typeface. There is also a standard naming convention throughout the book when explaining what to do in each step. The steps normally are something like this:

1. On the **Advanced Properties** page, select the **Confirm** check box, and then click **Next**.

Code and sample scripts are formatted like the following example, on a grey background.

```
DoNotCreateExtraPartition=YES
MachineObjectOU=ou=Workstations, dc=viamonstra, dc=com
```

The step-by-step guides in this book assume that you have configured a lab environment according to the information in Appendix A, "Lab Environment."

This book is not intended as a reference volume, covering every technology, feature, acronym, or command-line switch known to man, but rather is designed to make sure you learn what you need to know to successfully deploy, configure, and manage Windows 8 in an enterprise environment.

Sample Files

All sample files used in this book can be downloaded from www.deploymentfundamentals.com.

Additional Resources

In addition to all the tips and tricks provided in this book, you can find extra resources on my blog (www.theexperienceblog.com), like articles and even more tips and tricks drawn from issues I've encountered in real-world,.

Topics Not Covered

This book does not cover any of the consumer-targeted features of Windows 8.

Chapter 1

Setup, Installation, and Deployment

Deploying Windows 8 is not only a basic and necessary step for you to take, it is also a quite pleasant experience as the setup engine has been improved significantly in terms of performance. In this chapter, you learn what is necessary to deploy Windows 8 in an enterprise environment. The chapter also covers applications and hardware compatibility, which is a critical factor when you deploy a new Windows version, and some additional tools that you can use to aid in the deployment of Windows 8. Licensing and activation is another part of this chapter, as is the BIOS killer also known as UEFI (Unified Extensible Firmware Interface).

Architectures

Long before Microsoft had publicly announced Windows 8, there were rumors of a 128-bit Windows 8, with no 32-bit version and so forth. Forget everything you might have heard because now it's known that Windows 8 supports the exact same platform architectures as previous Windows versions with the addition of one new type of architecture.

Windows 8 is served in three flavors when it comes to architecture, with support for x86 (32-bit) platforms, x64 (64-bit) platforms, and, last but not least, the ARM type of processors.

Editions

With Windows 8, the number of editions available has been reduced for simplicity, compared with Windows Vista and Windows 7, which were delivered in a vast number of editions. The following are the available editions of Windows 8:

- Windows 8
- Windows 8 Pro
- Windows 8 Enterprise
- Windows RT

Basically, Windows 8 is the edition intended for home users whereas Windows 8 Pro is intended both for businesses and also for power users and enthusiasts. Although Windows 8 Pro contains basic business features, such as connecting it to a domain, there is no doubt that Windows 8 Enterprise is the real and only choice when dealing with Windows 8 in an enterprise.

The Enterprise version contains a lot of features which are imperative to the working of Windows 8 in an enterprise environment, especially when it comes to security and mobility. Therefore, the ViaMonstra Windows deployment covered in this book is for Windows 8 Enterprise.

Windows RT is Windows 8 for ARM-based devices. The primary differences between Windows RT and a "regular" Windows 8 edition is that Windows RT is not able to run x86 or x64 applications, and from an enterprise perspective, you are not able to join it to a domain. Although there are other ways to manage Windows 8 RT devices, it still lacks support for sideloading the modern-style apps introduced in Windows 8, and that makes the use of Windows 8 RT in enterprises somewhat limited. Due to the limitations in Windows RT, ViaMonstra chooses to deploy Windows 8 Enterprise on their slates instead of Windows RT.

Note: You can still find the special European edition of Windows 8, which comes without Windows media components. It is branded and known as the "N" edition.

Comparison

As this book is dealing with enterprises, I want to highlight the relevant differences between the two editions available for businesses. Basically, this means leaving out Windows RT and basic Windows 8, as those two editions are intended primarily for home users and a limited number of businesses.

Windows 8 Pro Features

- BitLocker and BitLocker To Go
- Boot from VHD
- Client Hyper-V

Note: Installing language packs and language interface packs to get Windows in another language is now available for all editions. Previously this was limited to the Enterprise and Ultimate editions of Windows Vista and Windows 7.

Windows 8 Enterprise Features

Note that all of the features in Windows 8 Pro are included in the Enterprise edition, plus the following ones:

- AppLocker
- BranchCache
- DirectAccess
- Modern-style app sideloading
- VDI support with RemoteFX
- Windows To Go

Summary of Windows 8 Editions

To summarize the editions and features, it is apparent that Microsoft has added some features to the Windows 8 Pro edition that previously were exclusive to Enterprise and Ultimate users. Those include BitLocker, BitLocker To Go, language packs, and Boot from VHD.

In Windows 8 Enterprise, you will find features such as DirectAccess, Windows To Go, AppLocker, and other features that are adding more value to the company as an enterprise client.

Compatibility

The most important thing when migrating to a newer operating system version is compatibility. How will everything that is working on my Windows platform today continue to work on the next version of Windows?

Starting with Windows Vista, which launched in 2007, Microsoft introduced a lot of major changes that significantly affected application and hardware compatibility when moving from Windows XP. Although things are improving on the application side, many enterprises still have a lot of old applications not compatible with the newer operating systems such as Windows Vista, Windows 7, or Windows 8.

Those of you who have moved from Windows XP to Windows 7 know what a really big challenge that move is in terms of compatibility.

Microsoft Focus on Maintaining Compatibility

One of Microsoft's Windows 8 focus areas has been maintaining compatibility to ease the transition for enterprises and promising a nearly 100-percent compatibility rate with Windows 7. This in practice means that if you are running Windows 7 today, you have a very good chance of moving to Windows 8 without any major problems at all.

If you are still on Windows XP, however, you will very likely encounter quite a few compatibility issues when moving to Windows 8. Luckily there are free Microsoft tools out there to aid in identifying potential problems, as well as fixing compatibility problems as they arise.

Compatibility Center

As with previous versions of Windows, Microsoft provides a web site that contains not only software compatibility information but also hardware compatibility statuses for Windows 8, both in x86 and x64 flavors of the operating system. This is one source of information for checking whether a particular piece of software or hardware works with or is certified for Windows 8. This compatibility status database is good for mainstream applications and hardware but will not cover all your applications and hardware. It is a good place to look, however. The Windows 8 compatibility center is available at http://www.microsoft.com/en-us/windows/compatibility/en-US/CompatCenter/Home.

Application Compatibility

Without working applications, you simply cannot move to a new Windows platform. Microsoft did put a lot of effort into making certain that application compatibility for businesses is better than ever in Windows 8. The end result is almost one-to-one application compatibility with Windows 7, but as already mentioned, you still have a challenge ahead of you if you are moving from Windows XP.

	Windows 7 x86	**Windows 8 x86**	**Windows 7 x64**	**Windows 8 x64**
Number of app compatibility fixes:	6568	7176	151	348

The number of application compatibility fixes has increased in Windows 8 compared to a fully patched Windows 7 SP1 machine (as of September 2012). Hundreds of fixes have been added to Windows 8.

Visual Basic 6 (VB6) Compatibility Remains the Same

In enterprises, there are still a lot of VB6 applications in use. It is interesting to note, and totally in line with Microsoft's 100-percent compatibility rate with Windows 7, is that VB6 is still supported in Windows 8 (as it is in Windows 7, I might add). Please note that not all VB6 components are included by default or supported in Windows 8. The recommendation is to include VB6 components with applications needing those particular VB6 components.

Note: Full details on which VB6 components are included with Windows 8, which ones you have to ship along with the applications, and which are not supported in Windows 8 can be found on the MSDN web site at http://msdn.microsoft.com/en-us/vstudio/ms788708.aspx.

Internet Explorer Compatibility

Although in most cases traditional applications will work without any problems in Windows 8, I have learned that there is one area that actually does not deliver as well on the compatibility side. That is web sites in Internet Explorer 10, which is the default browser in Windows 8. The problems I have seen are mostly related to visual flaws that can be worked around by setting the necessary compatibility flags in the code or in the browser.

Compatibility Mode Gets You There

You are still able to fall back to compatibility mode for previous versions of Internet Explorer by pressing F12 to reach the developer tools. From there, you can test your web site by choosing another Browser mode as well as Standard mode to see what is required for your web application.

Note: The default setting in Internet Explorer 8 and later is that all sites in the Intranet site zone are displayed in compatibility mode. This makes things seem to be working well, but you still should fix the code problems because they will likely cause problems sooner or later.

The behavior of a particular web application can be set in the web application code between the
<HEAD> and </HEAD> tags for the application. For example, you can use the following code for
Internet Explorer 10 and beyond:

```
<meta http-equiv="X-UA-Compatible" content="IE=Edge" />
```

Setting the **IE=Edge** tag makes sure that the web site is always rendered in native mode, which
with this particular meta string displays the web site in Internet Explorer 10 mode in Windows 8.
When, or if, Internet Explorer 11 is released, the sites using this tag will be rendered in IE11
mode.

To set the compatibility mode to previous versions of Internet Explorer, you can change this to a
previous version:

```
<meta http-equiv="X-UA-Compatible" content="IE=EmulateIE7" />
```

Setting the HTML compatibility tag in the web application will get the web application running in
many cases. However, I strongly recommend fixing the code problem, as that is a much better
solution in the long run. You will have a smoother upgrade to the next version of Internet Explorer
(or any other browser) if you make sure your applications are coded properly and according to
standards.

Real World Note: One example I encountered was a web application which actually had set IE to
support the absolutely latest standards, i.e. IE=Edge. However, the web application worked very
badly in Internet Explorer 10. On the other hand, it worked like a charm in Internet Explorer 9, so
setting the emulation mode to IE=EmulateIE9 made the application work until a more permanent
solution could be developed and implemented.

IE10 Compat Inspector

The Internet Explorer Compat Inspector tool is a really good way to quickly identify problems
with web applications. You simply add a line of code to the source of your web page, and it
identifies any possible compatibility issues it encounters and offers more information on how to
fix it.

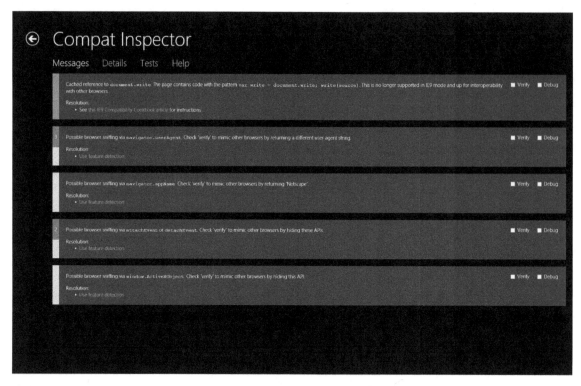

IE Compat Inspector is very easy to implement, and it will guide you to the problems it finds in your web applications so that you can solve them.

Note: You will find a step-by-step guide on troubleshooting your web applications at the Internet Explorer blog, http://blogs.msdn.com/b/ie/archive/2012/01/20/ie10-compat-inspector.aspx.

Hardware Compatibility

The compatibility situation with hardware is basically the same as with software: in almost all cases, what works today in Windows 7 will work with Windows 8. The rule of thumb when it comes to hardware, though, is that you need Windows 8-specific drivers for the best performance and to get the most out of features.

For instance, to gain the most out of graphics in Windows 8, you need a video card driver that is compatible with WDDM (Windows Display Driver Model) 1.2, which was introduced in Windows 8.

No More Windows XP Mode or MED-V

When Windows 7 was released, Microsoft needed a way to make sure that applications that just did not work in Windows 7 still were able to run on the Windows 7 platform via a virtual XP environment on each machine. Windows XP Mode was the standalone version, and MED-V (Microsoft Enterprise Desktop Virtualization) gave us that possibility as an enterprise solution.

As these tools mean significant overhead in terms of management and configuration, my recommendation is never to include them in any deployment project. So, I shed no tears when Microsoft announced that these tools would be discontinued as of Windows 8.

Instead, Microsoft gives us the Client Hyper-V feature which can be used to host guest operating systems of earlier Windows versions on Windows 8 machines, although without the integration the MED-V solution actually provided. By "integration," I mean the possibility of publishing shortcuts from the host OS to applications running in a virtual Windows XP machine on the host. With MED-V, you also can control that some URLs opened in the browser on the host instead open in the browser in the virtual machine. Client Hyper-V is covered in detail in Chapter 5.

Tools to Assess

To assist you with deploying a new operating system, Microsoft provides a number of free tools, so-called *solution accelerators*. I will take you through the most important tools when assessing and deploying Windows 8.

Assessment and Deployment Kit (ADK)

Some of you are certainly familiar with WAIK (Windows Automated Installation Kit). For those of you who are not, I can tell you that WAIK contains the most fundamental tools for dealing with operating system deployment. With Windows 8, WAIK has been rebranded and replaced by the Assessment and Deployment Kit (ADK).

The ADK also contains fundamental Windows deployment tools and components, plus it includes more tools like Windows Performance Toolkit, Windows Assessment Toolkit, the Volume Activation Management Tool (VAMT), and the Application Compatibility Toolkit (ACT) that were previously available as separate downloads.

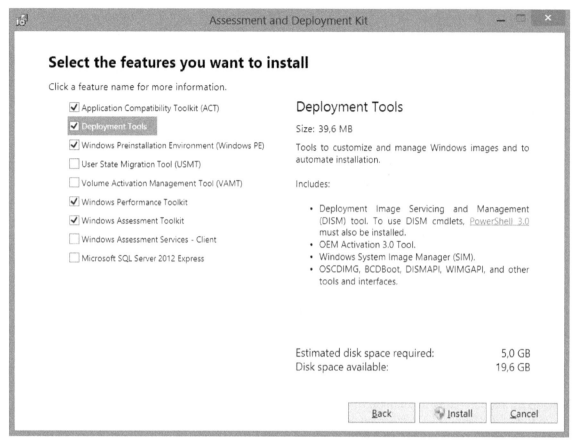

ADK contains the fundamental deployment tools, as well as tools to assess compatibility and performance.

Application Compatibility Toolkit (ACT)

One tool you cannot do without when migrating to a new Windows version is ACT. With this tool, you perform mainly three tasks: inventorying, testing, and fixing applications. ACT is included in the ADK. You can also install SQL Server Express 2012 from the ADK, which is needed when you do inventorying in ACT.

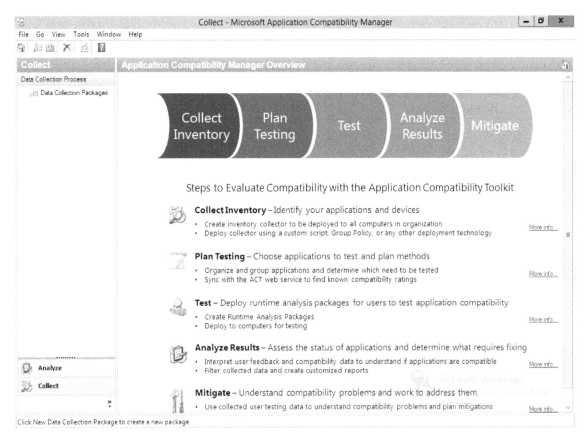

In ACT you can inventory and test application and mitigate application problems.

Inventorying

The basics of ACT when it comes to inventorying are creating an inventory package, deploying that package, waiting for data to be sent back from your client machines, and finally processing that data into the database so that you have data to work with.

> **Note:** This is the first lab in the book, so make sure that you have prepared the machines according to Appendix A, which contains all the information needed on setting up the lab environment. Of course, you also can use your own existing environment but do so at your own risk.

Configure Application Compatibility Toolkit

1. On **DC01**, log on as **Administrator** in the **VIAMONSTRA** domain.

2. Using **File Explorer**, create the **C:\ACTLogs** folder.

3. Using **File Explorer**, allow the **Domain Computers** group **Create files / write data** and **Create folders / append data** permissions (NTFS Permissions) to the **C:\ACTLogs** folder.

> **Note:** These are special permissions you set from the Advanced permissions view (click the **Show advanced permissions** link).

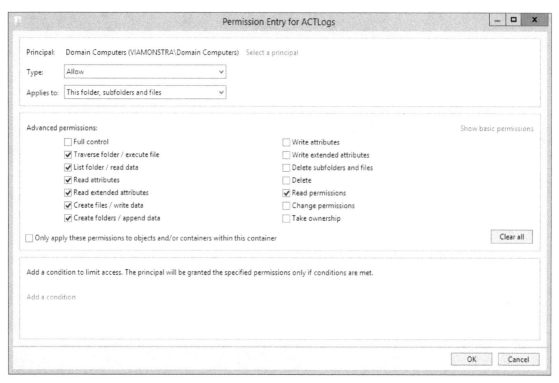

The Advanced permissions for the C:\ACTLogs folder·

4. On the **Start screen**, select the **Application Compatibility Manager**.

5. On the **Welcome to the ACT Configuration Wizard** page, click **Next**.

6. On the **Do you want to use this computer to run ACT Log Processing Service** page, select the **Yes** option, and then click **Next**.

7. On the **Configure Your ACT Database Settings** page, in the **SQL Server** text box, type **DC01\ADK** and click **Connect**.

8. In the **Database** text box, type **ACT** and then click **Next**.

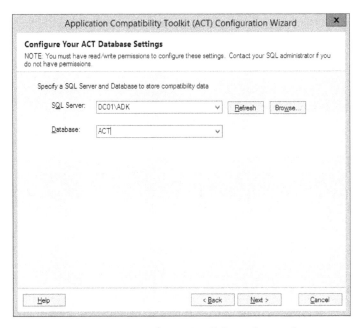

The first Configure Your ACT Database Settings page·

9. On the second **Configure Your ACT Database Settings** page, click **Next**.

10. On the **Configure Your Log File Location** page, use the following settings, and then click **Next**:

    a. Path: **C:\ACTLogs**

    b. Share as: **ACTLogs$**

11. On the **Configure Your ACT Log Processing Service Account** page, accept the default settings and click **Next**.

12. On the **Congratulations** page, accept the default settings and click **Finish**. The **Application Compatibility Manager** now starts.

Real World Note: If you don't have Internet access on the machine, you can clear the "Automatically check for updates on launch (recommended)" check box to speed up the start time of the Application Compatibility Manager.

Create the Inventory Package

1. In the **Application Compatibility Manager** console, click **Data Collection Packages** and double-click in the large white area where it says **Double-click to add a new Data Collection Package**.

2. On the **Choose the Type of Package to Create** page, click **Inventory collection package**.

3. On the **Set Up Your Inventory Package** page, accept the default settings and click **Create**.

4. In the **Save Data Collection Package** dialog box, browse to **C:\ACTLogs** and save the package there.

5. When the save is done, click **Finish** but do not close the **Application Compatibility Manager** console.

> **Note:** Information about installed applications is gathered from a number of common sources on a machine. If you choose to do runtime analysis, there is also an agent which runs on the machine for the time you specify. The agent reports back detailed information about how the applications running on the machine behave, for example, in terms of likely User Account Control (UAC) problems or applications using deprecated components.

Deploy the Inventory Package

1. On **CL01**, log on as **Administrator** in the **VIAMONSTRA** domain.

2. Press the **Windows logo key + R**, type **\\DC01\ACTLogs$**, and then press **Enter**.

3. Double-click **New_Package1.msi** to start the installation.

> **Note:** The installation will proceed and finish without notice, so do not think there is a problem due to this behavior. The inventory package is normally deployed by other means, such as your regular deployment tool for applications rather than installed manually.

Analyze the Data

1. Switch back to **DC01** (logged in as **Administrator** in the **VIAMONSTRA** domain).

2. In the **Application Compatibility Manager** console, click the **Analyze** tab.

3. In the **Windows 8 Reports** node, select the **Applications** node and have a peek around.

4. Still in the **Windows 8 Reports** node, select the **Internet Explorer Add-ons** node and have a peek around to see that you also can inventory browser add-ons and check their compatibility status.

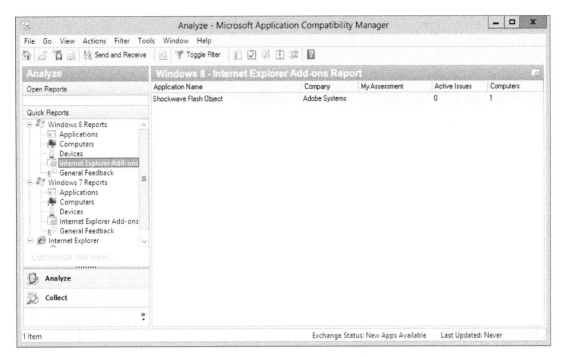

The Internet Explorer Add-ons node, showing the Shockwave Flash Object.

Testing

The testing phase basically consists of determining which applications to bring to the Windows 8 platform and then prioritizing them. A good feature of ACT is that it enables you to send and receive compatibility information from Microsoft's central compatibility database, including what other users have learned and reported in their migration projects.

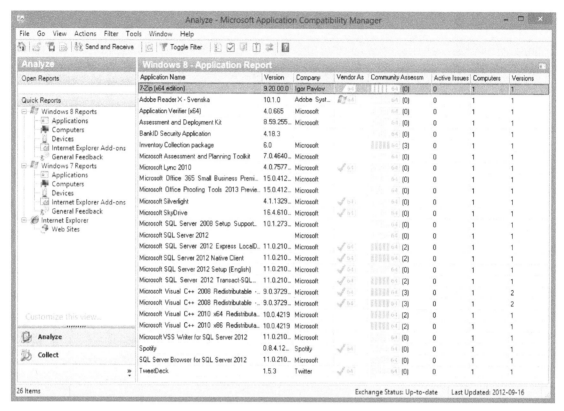

Applications and their compatibility status for Windows 8.

Fixing

During the actual application testing, you have to troubleshoot any errors that arise. There are a number of great tools to use when it comes to troubleshooting and finding out how to fix application problems. A couple of tools which I use frequently are:

- **Process Monitor.** The famous Sysinternals tool to gather exactly what is happening on a machine.

- **Dependency Walker.** Used to load DLL and OCX files to determine any dependencies they have to other resources.

Standard User Analyzer Tool

Included in ACT is a tool called Standard User Analyzer (SUA) tool, which you can use to further analyze any problems that exist in an application. The basic steps for using this tool are:

1. Install **ADK** on the Windows client on which you want to test applications.

2. Start the **Standard User Analyzer** tool (SUA.exe) from the **C:\Program Files (x86)\Windows Kits\8.0\Assessment and Deployment Kit \Application Compatibility Toolkit\Standard User Analyzer** folder.

3. Browse for and then launch the application you are testing.

4. Do whatever you (or preferably a user who knows the application) normally do and then exit the application.

5. Note whatever problems are listed and possibly use these to create so-called *shims* to your applications to make them work better in Windows 8.

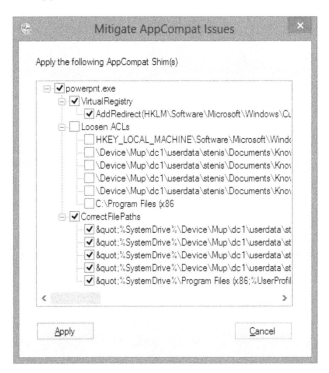

The Standard User Analyzer tool gives you suggested fixes, which can be applied as shims.

Real World Note: There are various workarounds for fixing problems, but the best solution in the long run is to fix the actual problem and not work around it.

Microsoft Assessment and Planning (MAP) Toolkit

From a Windows 8 perspective, the Microsoft Assessment and Planning (MAP) Toolkit will assist you in several ways: assessing hardware to see which machines will be able to run Windows 8, giving you insight into what applications you have installed, and indicating which drivers you will need to be on the lookout for that are not included on the Windows 8 installation media.

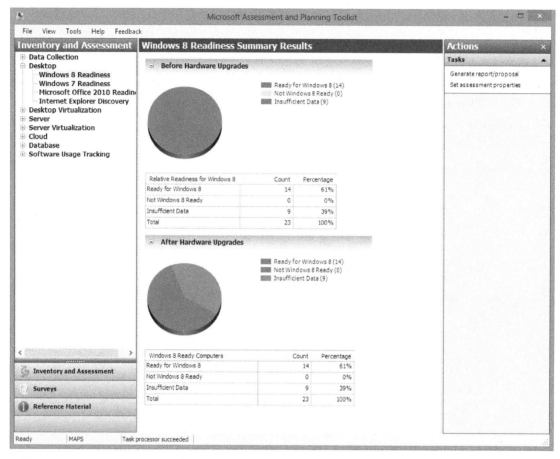

The MAP console after doing an inventory scan.

Doing an inventory with MAP consists of a scan, report generating, and finally an analyzing step.

Install MAP 7.0

1. On **CL01**, log in as **Administrator** in the **VIAMONSTRA** domain.

2. Mount the **Tools.iso** (located in the C:\ISO folder).

3. Start the **MAP 7.0 setup (D:\MAP 7.0 \Microsoft_Assessment_and_Planning_Toolkit_Setup.exe)**

4. On the **Welcome to the Microsoft Assessment and Planning Toolkit Setup Wizard** page, accept the default settings, and click **Next**.

5. On the **License Agreement** page, accept the license agreement and click **Next**.

6. On the **Installation Folder** page, accept the default settings and click **Next**.

7. On the **Customer Experience Improvement Program** page, select the **I don't want to join the program at this time** option, and click **Next**.

8. On the **Ready to Install** page, click **Install**.

9. On the **Installation Successful** page, accept the default settings, and click **Finish**. The **Microsoft Assessment and Planning Toolkit** console now opens with the configuration window.

The MAP 7.0 configuration window.

10. In the **Create or select a database** area, select the **Create an inventory database** option, assign a name of **MAP**, and click **OK**.

Perform the Inventory

1. In the **Microsoft Assessment and Planning Toolkit** console, under **Steps to complete**, next to **Perform an inventory**, click the **Go** button.

2. On the **Inventory Scenarios** page, explore the options, select the **Windows computers** scenario, and click **Next**.

3. On the **Discovery Methods** page, explore the options, accept the default settings, and then click **Next**.

4. On the **Active Directory Credentials** page, enter the following settings and click **Next** when done:

    a.   Domain: **viamonstra.com**

    b.   Domain account: **VIAMONSTRA\Administrator**

    c.   Password: **Pa$$w0rd**

5. On the **Active Directory Options** page, accept the default settings and then click **Next**.

6. On the **All Computers Credentials** page, click **Create**.

7. In the **Account Entry** window, enter the following information followed by **Save** and then **Next**:

    a.   Account name: **VIAMONSTRA\Administrator**

    b.   Password: **Pa$$w0rd**

    c.   Confirm password: **Pa$$w0rd**

8. On the **Credentials Order** page, accept the default settings and then click **Next**.

9. On the **Summary** page, click **Finish** to start the inventory.

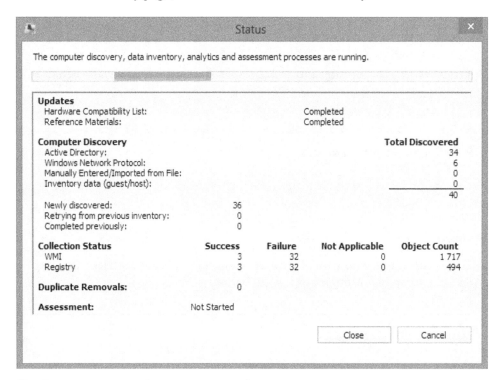

Performing a scan for computer objects to inventory.

Generate the Reports

1. In the **Microsoft Assessment and Planning Toolkit** console, in the left pane, expand **Desktop** and then select **Windows 8 Readiness**.

2. In the **Actions** pane on the right, under the **Tasks** menu, click **Set assessment properties**.

3. Take note of what customization options you have for a hardware assessment and click **Cancel**.

4. In the **Tasks** menu, click **Generate report/proposal**. Wait for the report generator to finish.

5. When the report is done, click **Close**.

Analyze the Data

1. In the **Microsoft Assessment and Planning Toolkit** console, in the **View** menu, select **Saved Reports and Proposals**.

2. Copy the files in the **C:\Users\Administrator.VIAMONSTRA\Documents\MAP\MAP** folder to a machine where you have Microsoft Office or the Word and Excel viewers installed.

3. On that machine, open each report file located there and investigate the information you get from these files.

Deploying Windows 8

Way too often, I see businesses that are trying or have tried to build their very own deployment solutions based on the standard tools that Microsoft provides as a part of the ADK (previously WAIK). My advice on doing Windows deployment is the following: Do not reinvent the wheel when doing deployments of Windows. Microsoft provides you with free solutions that will get you started doing fully automated deployments and reference images in minutes. You use the Microsoft Deployment Toolkit to achieve this.

Microsoft Deployment Toolkit (MDT)

With Microsoft Deployment Toolkit (MDT), you get a complete and automatic deployment in a few steps, so there is no need to do any manual actions when creating reference images or deploying Windows 8 to production machines.

> **Note:** You also can use Microsoft Deployment Toolkit 2012 Update 1 to deploy other Windows versions than Windows 8, starting with Windows XP and Windows Server 2003 and later.

After first installing Microsoft Deployment Toolkit 2012 Update 1, you start the Deployment Workbench which is where you manage everything regarding the deployment. You also need to install WAIK, or preferably ADK, to be able to deploy Windows 8. MDT serves as a graphical user interface on top of the fundamental deployment tools which are part of WAIK and ADK.

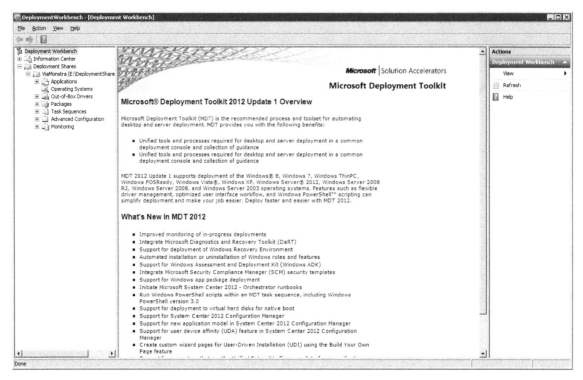

MDT 2012 Update 1 offers you a complete deployment solution for deploying Windows 8.

Creating a Fully Automated Network-Based Deployment Solution for Windows 8

In the real world, there is a need to accommodate for multiple scenarios when deploying an operating system. New machines that are purchased need to be re-imaged; you need to be able to reinstall (refresh) machines, as well as replacing machines with new ones. ViaMonstra has chosen to use network deployment using MDT in conjunction with Windows Deployment Services (WDS) to enable PXE network installation for all possible scenarios.

Create a Deployment Share

Before you can do anything creative at all in the Deployment Workbench, you need to create a deployment share, which basically is a shared folder, typically hosted on a server, which contains everything needed for deploying an operating system.

1. On **DC01**, log in as **Administrator** in the **VIAMONSTRA** domain.

2. On the **Start screen**, start the **Deployment Workbench**, right-click **Deployment Shares**, and choose **New Deployment Share**. The **New Deployment Share Wizard** opens.

3. On the **Path** page, accept the default settings and click **Next**.

4. On the **Share** page, accept the default settings and click **Next**.

5. On the **Descriptive Name** page, accept the default settings and click **Next**.

6. On the **Options** page, accept the default settings and click **Next**.

7. On the **Summary** page, accept the default settings and click **Next**.

8. On the **Confirmation** page, accept the default settings and click **Finish**.

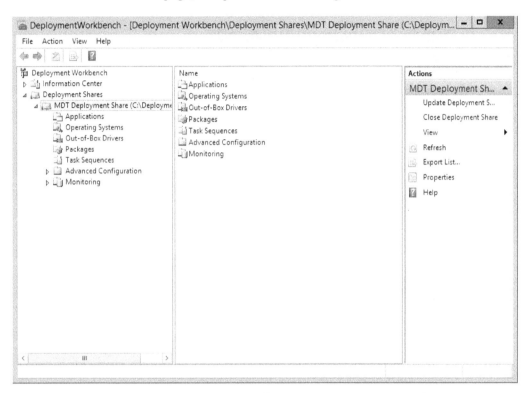

The deployment share contains all OS images, applications, drivers, language packs, or whatever you want to add to your deployment solution.

Import the Operating System

Next you need something to deploy, and what would be more appropriate than Windows 8 Enterprise x64? So you need to make sure that you have an installation DVD or an extracted or mounted ISO of Windows 8 Enterprise x64 available.

1. In the **Deployment Workbench**, expand the **Deployment Shares** node, and then expand the **MDT Deployment Share** node.

2. Right-click the **Operating Systems** node and select **Import Operating System**.

3. On the **OS Type** page, make sure the **Full set of source files** option is selected and click **Next**.

4. On the **Source** page, click **Browse** and point to the location of your extracted Windows 8 installation source files; then click **Next**.

5. On the **Destination** page, accept the default name and click **Next**.

6. On the **Summary** page, click **Next**.

7. On the **Confirmation** page, click **Finish**.

8. After the import, in the **Operating Systems** node, right-click the newly added operating system, select **Rename**, and assign the following name:

   Windows 8 Enterprise x64 default image

> **Real World Note:** The default .wim extension in the name is not needed. The operating system name in Deployment Workbench is just a logical representation.

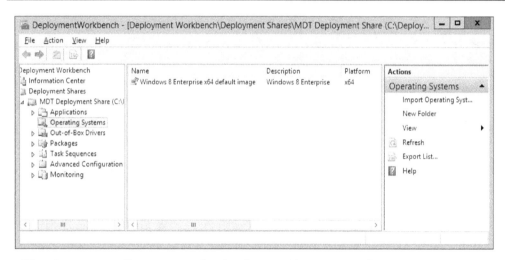

The Operating Systems node displaying the renamed operating system.

Create the Task Sequence

Now you have something to deploy, but you also need something that will tell the Windows setup what do to and in what order. This is why you need to create a task sequence.

1. In the **Deployment Workbench**, right-click the **Task Sequences** node and select **New Task Sequence**.

2. On the **General** page, use the following settings and then click **Next**:

   a. Task sequence ID: **W8**

   b. Task sequence name: **Windows 8 Enterprise x64**

3. On the **Select Template** page, make sure that **Standard Client Task Sequence** is selected and click **Next**.

4. On the **Select OS** page, select the **Windows 8 Enterprise x64 default image** operating system and click **Next**.

5. On the **Specify Product Key** page, accept the default setting and click **Next**.

6. On the **OS Settings** page, use the following settings and then click **Next**:

    a. Full Name: **Windows User**

    b. Organization: **ViaMonstra Inc.**

7. On the **Admin Password** page, enter the password **Pa$$w0rd** twice and click **Next**.

8. On the **Summary** page, click **Next**.

9. On the **Confirmation** page, click **Finish**.

10. In the **Task Sequence** node, double-click the **Windows 8 Enterprise x64** task sequence, and select the **Task Sequence** tab. Review the various actions.

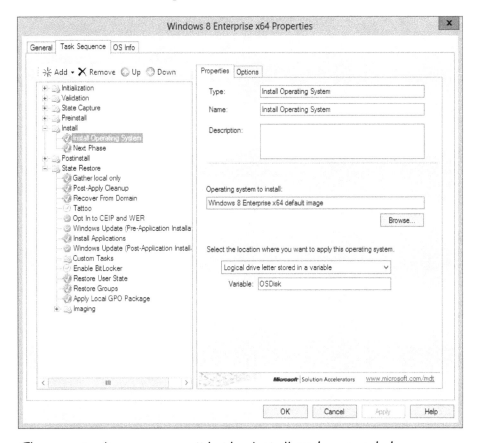

The new task sequence, with the Install node expanded.

The beauty of task sequences is that you can do a lot of customizations and you also can add dynamic driver schemes, language packs, hotfixes, applications, and much more to do really advanced deployments, still automatic and customized.

25

Customize the Rules

For the deployment to be fully automated, you need to add a few things to your rules (also called CustomSettings.ini).

1. In the **Deployment Workbench**, to edit **CustomSettings.ini**, right-click **MDT Deployment Share** and select **Properties**.

2. On the **Rules** tab, make sure that your settings match the following ones exactly:

> **Note:** If you don't like typing lots of text, you can find a copy of this CustomSettings.ini file in the book sample files.

```
[Settings]
Priority=Default

[Default]
OSInstall=Y
SkipCapture=YES
SkipAdminPassword=YES
AdminPassword=Pa$$w0rd
SkipProductKey=YES
SkipComputerBackup=YES
SkipUserData=YES
SkipBitLocker=YES
HideShell=YES
SkipSummary=YES
SkipLocaleSelection=YES
KeyboardLocale=en-us
UserLocale=en-us
TimeZoneName=W. Europe Standard Time
SkipTimeZone=YES
SkipComputerName=YES
OSDComputerName=CL02
SkipDomainMembership=YES
JoinDomain=viamonstra.com
DomainAdmin=VIAMONSTRA\Administrator
DomainAdminPassword=Pa$$w0rd
MachineObjectOU=OU=Workstations,DC=viamonstra,DC=com
```

3. Then click the **Edit Bootstrap.ini** button and make sure that the contents of Bootstrap.ini match the following:

Note: Again, if you don't like typing, you can find a copy of this Bootstrap.ini file in the book sample files.

```
[Settings]
Priority=Default

[Default]
SkipBDDWelcome=YES
DeployRoot=\\DC01\DeploymentShare$
UserDomain=VIAMONSTRA
UserID=Administrator
UserPassword=Pa$$w0rd
```

Update the Deployment Share

The last thing to do is to update the deployment share, which will take settings from your Bootstrap.ini file and put them into both a bootable ISO file and a WIM file that you can use to deploy Windows 8.

1. In the **Deployment Workbench**, right-click **MDT Deployment Share** and select **Update deployment share**.

2. On the **Options** page, accept the default settings and click **Next**.

3. On the **Summary** page, click **Next**. Wait several minutes until the boot images have been updated.

4. On the **Confirmation** page, click **Finish**.

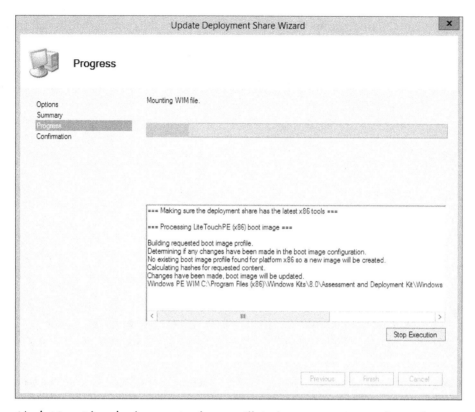

Updating the deployment share will take some time when there are new changes to include in the boot images·

Configuring the Network Installation Environment

Next you need to configure the Windows Deployment Services so you can do a network PXE boot when installing your Windows 8 client machines.

1. On **DC01**, log in as **Administrator** in the **VIAMONSTRA** domain.

2. Using **Sever Manager**, select the **Tools** menu, and select **Windows Deployment Services**.

3. In the **Windows Deployment Services** console, expand the **Servers** node.

4. Right-click **DC01.viamonstra.com**, select **Configure Server**, and complete the **Windows Deployment Services Wizard** using the following settings:

    a. On the **Before You Begin** page, click **Next**.

    b. On the **Install Options** page, accept the default settings and click **Next**.

    c. On the **Remote Installation Folder Location** page, accept the default settings and click **Next**. Then click **Yes** in the **System Volume Warning** dialog box that appears.

d.   On the **Proxy DHCP Server** page, accept the default settings and click **Next**.

e.   On the **PXE Server Initial Settings** page, select **Respond to all client computers (known and unknown)** and then click **Next**.

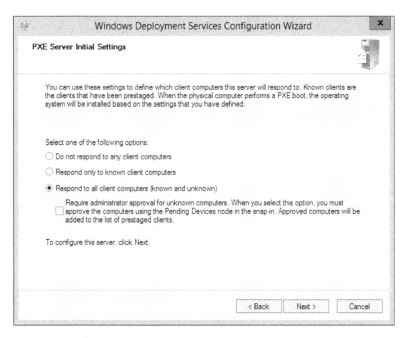

The PXE Server Initial settings page·

f.   On the **Task Progress** page, click **Finish**.

Note: If the Windows Deployment Service doesn't start directly via the wizard, start it manually through the Windows Deployment Service console or Services in the Control Panel.

5.   In the **Windows Deployment Services** console, expand **DC01.viamonstra.com** and click **Boot Images**.

6.   Right-click **Boot Images**, select **Add Boot Image**, and complete the **Add Image Wizard** using the following settings:

a.   In the **File location** input field, select **Browse**.

b.   Browse to **C:\DeploymentShare\Boot** and select **LiteTouchPE_x64.wim**; then select **Open** and click **Next**.

c.   On the **Image Metadata** page, accept the default settings and click **Next**.

d.   On the **Summary** page, click **Next**.

e.   When the import is done, click **Finish** and close the **Windows Deployment Services** console.

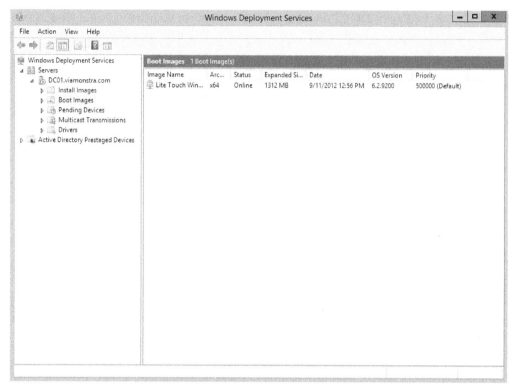

The Lite Touch boot image in WDS is all you need to start deploying Windows 8. The boot image will launch WinPE and connect to your deployment share and install from there.

Deploying a Windows 8 Machine Using MDT 2012 Update 1

1. On the host machine, using **Hyper-V Manager**, create a virtual machine with the following settings:

   a. Name: **CL02**

   b. Location: **C:\VMs**

   c. Memory: **2048 MB**

   d. Network: **Internal**

   e. Hard disk: **127 GB** (dynamic disk)

   f. Installation options: **Install an operating system from a network-based installation server.**

2. Start the **CL02** virtual machine, and allow it to PXE boot.

> **Note:** Make sure to be on the alert and press **F12** when **CL02** makes contact with the PXE/WDS server. You need to be quick. ☺

```
Hyper-V
PXE Network Boot 09.14.2011
(C) Copyright 2011 Microsoft Corporation, All Rights Reserved.


CLIENT MAC ADDR: 00 15 5D 0A 91 38  GUID: 2E99FC13-C6E1-429E-8ADC-2F5CD1C651BD
CLIENT IP: 192.168.0.201  MASK: 255.255.255.0  DHCP IP: 192.168.0.100
GATEWAY IP: 192.168.0.254

Downloaded WDSNBP from 192.168.0.100 DC01.viamonstra.com

Press F12 for network service boot
_
```

The PXE boot process on CL02.

3. Watch WinPE load and then see Microsoft Deployment Toolkit initiate.

4. To install Windows 8, select the task sequence named **Windows 8 Enterprise x64**, click **Next**, and watch the installation start. Although the Windows 8 setup and installation routine is really fast, the deployment will take some time.

> **Note:** For purposes of the demonstration, I did not automate the task sequence selection. You can skip the step for selecting the task sequence by adding the following variable lines in the rules (CustomSettings.ini):
>
> SkipTaskSequence=YES
> TaskSequenceID=W8

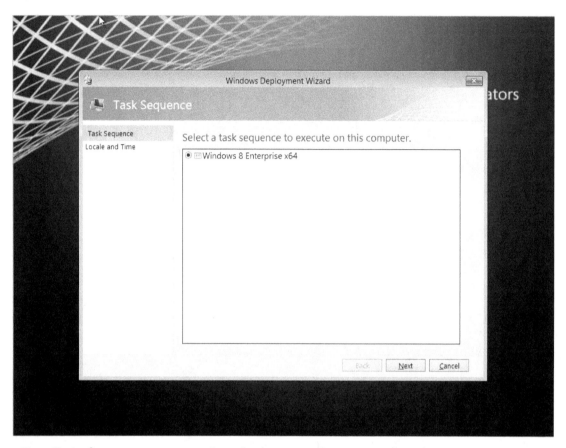

The Task Sequence page in the Windows Deployment Wizard.

Other Deployment Options

Microsoft Deployment Toolkit combined with Windows Deployment Services provides a really good deployment solution suitable for many companies. In larger enterprises, you will likely see benefits in using the big brother of tools, System Center Configuration Manager, which by the way uses Microsoft Deployment Toolkit and the exact same principles of using task sequences, operating system images, boot images, and so on.

> **Real World Note:** The book *Deployment Fundamentals, Volume 4: Deploying Windows 8 and Office 2013 Using MDT 2012 Update 1* covers all you need to know about deploying Windows 8 (and Office 2013) using Microsoft Deployment Toolkit 2012 Update 1. It is written by two of the world's most foremost experts on deployments, Johan Arwidmark and Mikael Nyström.

Licensing and Activation

I don't think anyone considers licensing and activation to be fun. There is nothing much to say about it because you need your machines to be both licensed and activated. Most enterprise environments running Windows 7 (or Windows Server 2008 R2) have a Key Management Service (KMS) server setup that will activate machines automatically.

Windows 8 introduces a new way of activating client machines: that is, Active Directory-based activations. You also can do KMS-based activations like before, or use Multiple Activation Key (MAK) activation for scenarios in which you do not have at least 25 machines to activate (the KMS-based activation minimum).

Active Directory-Based Activation vs. KMS Activation

Active Directory-Based Activation (ADBA) basically means easier and more secure activation than ever. Having the activation done via the regular communication with domain controllers requires the machine to be a part of the domain, meaning you have total control over which machines can be activated in your environment.

The really small business will benefit from the fact that you can skip MAK activation and rely solely on ADBA for Windows 8, as there are no limits on the number of clients you need to have.

Requirements for Using ADBA

To be able to use ADBA, you must extend the Active Directory schema to a Windows Server 2012 schema. This does not mean you need to introduce Windows Server 2012 domain controllers in your environment, but you need to take the adprep utility from the Windows Server 2012 installation media (located in the support/adprep directory) and run that command from any domain member in the domain. This extends the schema of the Active Directory to house the new activation objects.

> **Note:** To be able to use an existing Windows Server 2008 R2 KMS server to activate Windows 8 clients, you must install the hotfix found in http://support.microsoft.com/kb/2691586.

Coexistence with Your Current KMS Infrastructure

In an enterprise environment, you most likely already have a KMS infrastructure activating not only your Windows 7 machines but also Office 2010. That is the case for ViaMonstra. The point is that if you do have KMS in place, you can and must continue to use KMS to be able to activate Windows 7 and Office 2010 for as long as you have these products in your environment. ADBA is applicable only for Windows 8, Windows Server 2012, and Office 2013.

Volume Activation Role

Previously there has been no elegant (read GUI) way of activating a KMS server. Starting with Windows Server 2012, there is a new role made specifically for activation. It is called the Volume Activation role.

Install Volume Activation

1. On **DC01**, log in as **Administrator** in the **VIAMONSTRA** domain.

2. Using **Server Manager**, select **Add roles and features**.

3. On the **Select installation type** page, select the **Role-based or feature-based installation** option and click **Next**.

4. On the **Select destination server** page, verify that **DC01.viamonstra.com** is selected and click **Next**.

5. On the **Select server roles** page, select the **Volume Activation Services** role.

6. In the **Add Roles and Features Wizard** dialog box, select **Add Features** and then click **Next**.

7. On the **Select features** page, accept the default settings and click **Next**.

8. On the **Volume Activation Services** page, click **Next**.

9. On the **Confirm installation selections** page, click **Install**.

10. When the installation is finished, click **Close**.

Real World Note: In non-Windows Server 2012 environments, extending the schema to 2012 level without having Windows Server 2012 domain controllers requires the use of the Volume Activation Management Tool (VAMT). VAMT, which is a part of ADK, enables you to configure ADBA.

Configure Volume Activation

You need to configure how you want activation to take place and, in doing so, select whether to deploy a KMS or an ADBA configuration.

1. On **DC01**, log in as **Administrator** in the **VIAMONSTRA** domain.

2. In **Server Manager**, click **VA Services** in the left navigation pane.

3. In the yellow bar with the text **Configuration required for Volume Activation Services at DC01**, click the **More** link.

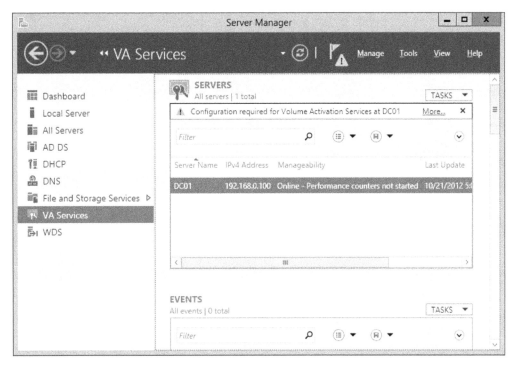

The VA Services node in Server Manager.

4. On the **All Servers Task Details** page, on the **Post-deployment configuration** line, click the **Volume Activation Tools** link.

5. On the **Select Volume Activation Method** page, choose **Active Directory-Based Activation** or **Key Management Service** option and then click **Next**.

6. On the **Manage Activation Objects** page, in the **Install your KMS host key** text box, type your KMS product key and click **Next**.

> **Note:** You need to have your KMS key at this point in time. Remember that when you install a KMS key on a Windows server, you cannot use the KMS key for a Windows client. So enter the KMS key of the Windows Server SKU, which also will activate your Windows clients.

7. On the **Activate Product** page, accept the default settings and click **Commit**.

8. On the **Volume Activation Tools** dialog box, click **Yes**.

9. On the **Activation Succeeded** page, click **Close**.

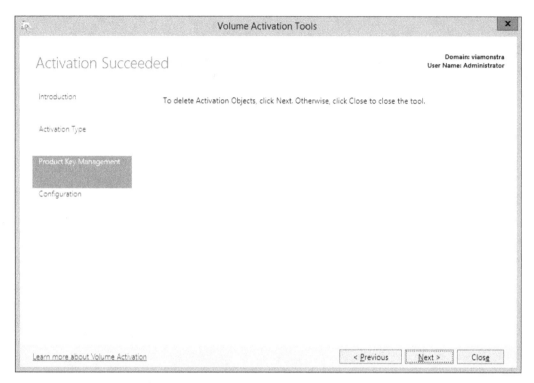

The Activation Succeeded page.

Performance Improvements

The same setup engine used since Windows Vista is used in Windows 8 to actually install the operating system. But you will definitely be glad to hear that performance for the setup engine has been improved dramatically.

I can say that setup and installation performance has been really good all along from the consumer preview and on. Here are installation times for Windows 8 compared to Windows 7.

Operating System and Architecture	Time to Deploy OS (minutes:seconds)
Windows 7 Enterprise x86 with SP1	8:02
Windows 8 Enterprise x86 RTM	5:37
Windows 8 Enterprise x64 RTM	6:11

Installation times are drastically reduced in Windows 8 compared to Windows 7.

Note: The test has been performed by using Microsoft Deployment Toolkit 2012 Update 1 to create a fully automated offline media. The installation times were measured from the start of the deployment until the deployment finished.

UEFI

BIOS has been around for decades and is in the process of being replaced completely by something called UEFI (Unified Extensible Firmware Interface). A few years from now (2012), all new machines will ship in UEFI mode only. What does this mean in terms of platform and compatibility? Well, to start with, it is only the 64-bit version of Windows that supports UEFI, and that has been the case on the client side since Windows Vista Service Pack 1 shipped.

Benefits of Using UEFI

To get the most out of Windows 8, you need to be using a piece of hardware that supports UEFI, in particular UEFI version 2.3.1. Here are some of the benefits of using Windows 8 on a UEFI-enabled machine:

- **Improved performance**. This depends on hardware and firmware, but performance when running Windows in UEFI mode is generally better than in BIOS mode as data is read in bigger chunks. A big performance saver is that the BIOS/OEM flash screen doesn't display for some number of seconds. Booting is instant on UEFI machines.

- **Support for new features**. BitLocker Network unlock, the ability to multicast boot PXE/boot images, and using Trusted Boot are features that all require UEFI to work.

- **Boot from large HD**. Only in UEFI mode is it possible to boot a machine that has a hard drive larger than 2.2 TB.

Partitioning Differs on BIOS and UEFI Systems

One fundamental difference between a machine running in legacy BIOS mode and in UEFI mode is how the drive is partitioned. In BIOS legacy mode, you typically have a boot partition (hidden from the user interface) and an operating system drive. In a UEFI installation, you have an EFI System partition and a boot partition, as well as an operating system partition.

What this means in practice is that you cannot just enable UEFI mode in the firmware (BIOS) and continue to run Windows. To be able to utilize UEFI, you must install the operating system in UEFI mode. This is typically done by first activating UEFI in the firmware and then installing Windows from a DVD or USB memory stick. When PXE becomes available for your hardware, that is also an option for deploying Windows 8 in UEFI mode.

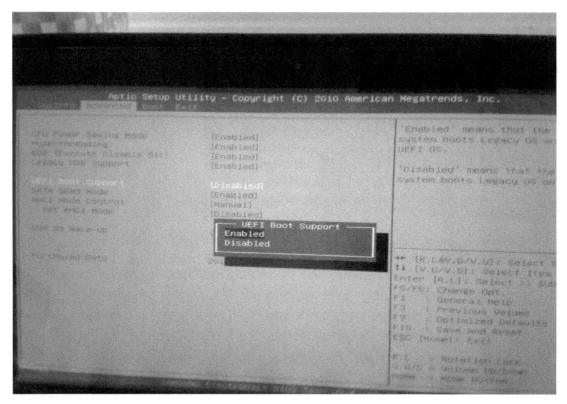

UEFI is never activated by default on legacy systems that are not Windows 8 certified so activating this manually is important if using UEFI.

When you choose to boot from a DVD or a USB memory stick, you will get a chance to boot from that device in UEFI mode. Then when you do the setup of Windows 8, it will automatically partition the device for UEFI mode.

> **Real World Note:** For most legacy systems (pre-Windows 8-certified hardware), there is no way to deploy machines in any automated fashion (i.e. PXE network boot) in UEFI mode. You need a UEFI driver for the network card, which hardware manufacturers typically do not provide for legacy systems.

How to Get Started with UEFI on Legacy Machines

Actually you probably already have a UEFI-enabled machine although you might not know it. Manufacturers have shipped machines with UEFI for years now, but unless it is a Windows 8-certified machine, UEFI is not enabled by default. Even if you do not have purely Windows 8-certified machines, you can enable UEFI on legacy machines and get started with Windows 8 in UEFI mode right away.

Activate UEFI Mode and Install Windows 8 in UEFI Mode

1. On a physical machine, enter **BIOS** setup instead of booting into Windows.

2. Change the boot mode from **Legacy** to **UEFI** or **UEFI compatible** mode. How you set this and the naming of this setting vary from vendor to vendor.

3. With the installation media on DVD or a USB memory stick inserted in the machine, boot the machine and bring up the boot menu, by pressing **F12** on many machines.

4. In the **UEFI** section, choose to boot from your media, DVD or USB memory stick, which will launch setup in UEFI mode and make the partitioning for UEFI mode correct.

5. When done installing Windows 8, you can start the tool **msinfo32.exe** from the **Start screen**, and look for the **Item** column for BIOS Mode. If you are in UEFI mode, it will say **UEFI**; if you are in BIOS mode, it will say **Legacy**.

Moving Forward

UEFI machines will become more and more common as Windows 8-certified machines come out, so remember that you cannot just switch to UEFI overnight, unless you can replace all your current hardware at once. Lucky you if that is not a problem. ☺

Chapter 2

User Interface and Apps

It used to be called the "Metro" interface but is now known just as the Windows 8 user interface. It is without a doubt the most controversial change in Windows since the Windows desktop and Start menu were introduced in Windows 95 quite a few years ago. This chapter covers the user interface and various aspects of it, such as how to deal with the two Internet Explorer browsers. It also deals with handling Windows 8 modern-style apps in an enterprise environment. This includes the so-called "sideloading" of the apps.

What Happened to the Start Menu?

I don't believe that the Start menu in Windows 8 is really that big of a deal. Let's take a second and think about what Microsoft actually has done to the Start menu. Number 1, the Start menu is now a larger, full-screen menu called the *Start screen*. Number 2, after logging in, you now land on the Start screen instead of the desktop.

Microsoft has done a lot of work to keep it that way, meaning that by default you are not able to bypass the Start screen and jump straight to the desktop. Although there are third-party products or tweaks you can use to get straight to the desktop, there are no official settings you can use to make the user land directly on the desktop.

> **Note**: As a side note, there was a Group Policy setting for going straight to the desktop after login in the Consumer Preview of Windows 8, which stated specifically that it was only intended for Windows Server 2012 (Windows Server 8 beta at that time).

Microsoft's standpoint on the Start screen is clear: you shall not and cannot bypass it (at least not very easily because there are various tricks for jumping to the desktop after all). On a pre-Windows 8 machine, what is the first thing a typical user does after logging in? I, and most users I have talked with, start something. It might be Outlook, a web browser, or any other application. Landing on the Start screen in that case means one less click to the application in question.

Also note that the classic Start button has been removed from the user interface. You can still find it by bringing the mouse cursor down to the left corner of the screen or via the charms.

The Start screen as seen right after a user login to a Windows 8 machine.

Touch Friendly and All

It's no secret that the new user interface is working really well and was developed for touch-based devices so it fit on all types of devices. But still what's all the fuss about it? The million-dollar question is how the new user interface works on a traditional desktop or laptop computer.

Using the new interface on a traditional form-based machine is pretty much the same as working with Windows 7. All line-of-business applications and most other applications, as well, are not the new Windows 8 apps, meaning they run on the desktop. So what happens when a user logs in is that the user starts something from the Start screen and thereby indirectly goes to the desktop mode.

When on the desktop, using Windows 8 is pretty much like using Windows 7, only better in a number of usability aspects. Whenever you need to find something or start a new application, you just press the Windows logo key and start typing. You are presented with search results and further actions to find what you are looking for.

Real World Note: Most of the things are actually easier to do in the new user interface, but shutting down the machine means a few more steps than I am comfortable with. Bringing out the good old Alt + F4 while on the desktop is the quickest way of shutting down or restarting a Windows 8 machine.

Basics for Using the New Interface

The Windows logo key has the exact same importance in Windows 8 as in previous Windows versions. Pressing the key brings up the Start screen where you can reach anything on the machine, let it be applications, settings, files, or other types of content.

Using the Windows Logo Key and the Charms

1. Press the **Windows logo key** to get to the Start screen.

2. Point your mouse cursor to the upper right or lower right corner to bring up the **charms**, which is a central part in Windows 8.

3. Explore what options you can find in the charms; start with **Search** and then have a look at the **Share**, **Devices**, and **Settings** charms.

The charms are reachable both from the Start screen and the new modern-style interface. Also take note that when you are running a particular modern-style app, opening the charms and choosing Settings brings up settings for that particular app. The charms and their contents are dynamic to some extent.

Note: You also can bring up the charms by pressing Windows logo key + C, or by swiping a finger in from the right on a touch-based device.

The charms brought out in desktop mode.

Search in the New Interface

Search has been a high-priority feature in each new modern Windows release, and Windows 8 is no different in that respect. The fact is that with the new search introduced in Windows 8 you will find what you want from a great number of sources in a unified interface. Search in Windows 8 is really powerful!

How to Do a Search in Windows 8

1. Press the **Windows logo key** to get to the Start screen.

2. Type **power** and watch the results. Note that **Apps** is marked in the search bar to the right.

3. Now click **Settings** to see only the settings related to **power**.

Note: If you have an active internet connection on your Windows 8 machine, you also can click any other app in the list in the search bar to get search results from within those apps.

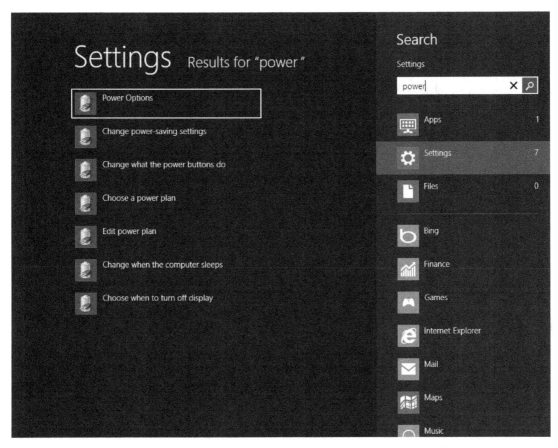

In Windows 8, you can do a search in a number of sources, including modern-style apps that honor the search framework.

Keyboard Shortcuts

The new Windows 8 user interface brings out some new keyboard shortcuts that are essential if you want to use Windows 8 in an efficient way.

- **Windows logo key**. Go straight to the Start screen.
- **Windows logo key + C**. Bring up the charms.
- **Windows logo key + W**. Go directly to search for settings.
- **Windows logo key + F**. Go directly to search for files.
- **Windows logo key + Q**. Bring up a list of all installed applications.

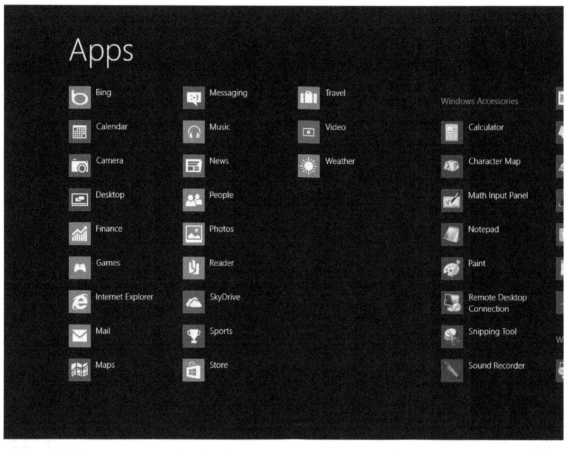

Windows logo key + Q opens a screen as close to the classic Start menu as you can get; it lists all apps and applications.

Power Menu

As an IT professional working with Windows 8, you will use some tools quite often when working with Windows clients. Microsoft actually did remove the Start button but left something hidden in the place where that button used to reside. That is what I call the "power menu," which is a great addition for IT professionals. Press the Windows logo key + X, and you will see it appear in the lower left corner of the screen.

You also can reach it by right-clicking in the lower left corner of the screen. That power menu contains a lot of the stuff you need to reach as an IT professional or enthusiast. Unfortunately, you cannot add your own shortcuts to this list in any recommended or supported way.

Programs and Features
Power Options
Event Viewer
System
Device Manager
Disk Management
Computer Management
Command Prompt
Command Prompt (Admin)

Task Manager
Control Panel
File Explorer
Search
Run

Desktop

Windows 8 Enterprise
Build 9200
6:05 AM
9/16/2012

Right-clicking in the lower left corner of the screen opens the "power menu."

Multiple Monitors

One thing that is quite common in enterprises, at least in the IT department and for developers, is having multiple monitors. Windows 8 works really well with dual monitors as it expands the taskbar and can have wide-screen dual-monitor desktop backgrounds. Moving applications between monitors makes the application active in the taskbar on that monitor, which is really nice. This is the default behavior, but the end user also can configure it via the taskbar properties.

As you know by now, the screen corners in Windows 8 are essential for reaching certain menus. When you have multiple monitors, you can reach the Windows 8 menus, such as the Start screen or charms, by pointing the mouse in the corner on any monitor. The corners are *hot*, meaning you do not precisely have to hit the 1x1 pixel that represent the corner. Instead, there is a somewhat larger active area, which makes the corners hot.

That way, in multi-monitor scenarios, you can reach the Start screen from any other screen, and you can have the modern-style UI running on monitor 1, while you working on the desktop on monitor 2, for instance.

Internet Explorer vs. Internet Explorer for the Desktop

Now that you are familiar with the basics of the user interface in Windows 8, let's dig into the Internet Explorer 10 web browser that is included in Windows 8. You might think that there are two browsers in Windows 8, but actually there is just one, at least technically speaking.

Internet Explorer 10 comes in two flavors:

- **Internet Explorer**. The IE browser that runs as a Windows 8 app inside the new Windows 8 user interface is called simply Internet Explorer.

- **Internet Explorer for the desktop**. If you go to the desktop in Windows 8 and launch Internet Explorer from the button on the taskbar, you reach Internet Explorer for the desktop.

Although they might look like two browsers, the core is the same, meaning that the rendering engine for web and JavaScript and all security foundations are the same regardless of whether you are browsing a site in the new Windows 8 user interface or on the desktop.

Internet Explorer is shown in full screen mode in the modern user interface.

Internet Explorer for the Desktop with the classic minimalist interface.

Flash Now Included in Internet Explorer

You will probably be glad to hear that Adobe Flash is now shipped in Windows 8. From an enterprise point of view, this means that you are able to patch Flash using your favorite patch tool, Windows Server Update Services. That is great news because it means you do not have to package (or re-package) and test Flash yourself using other deployment methods. Such methods take a significant amount of time, as new versions of Flash traditionally have been released rather frequently.

Plugins or No Plugins

The one most significant difference between Internet Explorer and Internet Explorer for the desktop is the ability to run plugins. In Internet Explorer for the desktop, you are allowed to run plugins, such as Adobe Flash, Java, Silverlight, and any ActiveX controls. When you run Internet Explorer in the Windows 8 user interface, you cannot use any plug-ins.

Flash Compatibility List

Of course, there is one exception to the plugin rule. Some sites actually do support using Adobe Flash in Internet Explorer. The sites that allow Flash are included in the "Internet Explorer compatibility list" that is distributed by Microsoft and houses compatibility modes for certain web sites. As of IE10, the list also has a section for sites that are allowed to use Flash in Internet Explorer 10.

As a web site owner, you can get on this list by contacting Microsoft at the email address iepo@microsoft.com and supplying basic information about your web site, including company name, contact information, and the site's URL. Analysis is done by Microsoft to verify that the site meets certain requirements in terms of performance and usability on multiple types of Windows 8 devices. If the site meets the requirements, it eventually will be included in the Flash section in the compatibility list.

Note: The contents of the compatibility list and all sites that are displayed in compatibility mode or allowed to use Flash content can be viewed in clear text by looking in the file iecompatdata.xml found in C:\Users\<username>\AppData\Local\Microsoft\Internet Explorer\IECompatData.

Setting the Base in the Enterprise

In my experience, the vast majority of web applications in enterprises depend on some kind of plugin, be it Java, Flash, or some ActiveX control. What this means in practice is that you want to control how URLs are dealt with in Windows 8. You want to do this because you do not want your users to open a web application in Internet Explorer only to see that it is not working because plugins are only allowed to run in Internet Explorer for the desktop.

You also do not want the hassle of some links opening in Internet Explorer for desktop and some in Internet Explorer. You want to keep it consistent and simple and keep your users happy.

A useful change is to make sure that when a user pins a website to or opens a URL shortcut from the Start screen, it opens in Internet Explorer for the desktop.

Make Sure That Web Applications Open in the Right Internet Explorer Application

1. On **DC01**, log in as **Administrator** in the **VIAMONSTRA** domain.
2. Using the **Group Policy Management** console, right-click the **Workstations** OU, and select **Create a GPO in this domain, and Link it here**.
3. Assign the name **Workstation Configuration** to the new group policy.
4. Expand the **Workstations** OU, right-click the **Workstation Configuration** group policy, and select **Edit**.

Note: The focus in this book is enterprise scenarios, which means you always use domain policies, even though most settings also can be configured on a single machine using the Local Group Policy Editor (gpedit.msc). You can chose to do GPO management from a domain controller or by installing the Remote Server Administration Tools (RSAT) and adding the Group Policy Management console to your client machine. See Chapter 7 for more information on RSAT.

5. Expand the **Computer Configuration** / **Policies** / **Administrative Templates** / **Windows Components** / **Internet Explorer** / **Internet Settings** node. (This setting can also be set for the user in User Configuration.)

6. Open the setting **Set how links are opening in Internet Explorer** and set it to **Enabled** and **Always in Internet Explorer on the desktop**.

7. Open the setting **Open Internet Explorer tiles on the desktop** and set it to **Enabled**.

Real World Note: Even though you can change these link settings in User Configuration, you might want to consider setting them in the computer configuration so that you can have one configuration for your desktops and laptops and one configuration for your potential slate devices, provided that you separate these devices using different OUs in Active Directory.

Removal of the Internet Explorer Maintenance Extension

If you are used to controlling Internet Explorer settings via the group policy extension Internet Explorer Maintenance, look no further. That part has been deprecated as of Internet Explorer 10 and Windows 8. The replacement for Internet Explorer Maintenance is either Group Policy preferences (GPP) or the Internet Explorer Administration Kit (IEAK) to create custom settings for Internet Explorer 10.

Note: A popular setting in Internet Explorer Maintenance is the proxy configuration. This is now set via IEAK. See the reference sheet for Internet Explorer Maintenance conversion to either GPP or IEAK at http://technet.microsoft.com/library/hh846772.aspx.

Enhanced Protected Mode

Protected mode for Internet Explorer was introduced in Windows Vista and has been there ever since. Is makes Internet Explorer run in a sort of sandbox with the lowest possible privileges to the system. This significantly reduces the attack surface for Internet Explorer.

In Windows 8, protected mode has been improved even further, and now Internet Explorer runs in *enhanced protected mode*. This is optional for Internet Explorer for the desktop, but it is activated by default for Internet Explorer running in the modern interface.

The downside if you activate enhanced protected mode is that not all plugins for Internet Explorer for the desktop are compatible with this new enhanced security feature. Effectively any add-on not compatible with it will be disabled.

On a 64-bit Windows 8 machine, Internet Explorer for the desktop launches the main process in 64-bit mode but loads all tabs in 32-bit mode to make sure that plugins work as expected because most of them are 32-bit only. On the other hand, when enhanced protected mode is activated for Internet Explorer in 64-bit Windows 8, all tabs load in 64-bit mode.

My recommendation is that before enabling enhanced protected mode, test to verify whether your web applications work as expected with the enhanced security. If you have 32-bit only add-ons, activating enhanced protected mode is not an option.

Note: If you turn off the infamous UAC (User Account Control), you also prevent Internet Explorer from running in protected mode. Learn more about UAC in Chapter 4.

How to Activate Enhanced Protected Mode

1. On **CL01**, log in as **Administrator** in the **VIAMONSTRA** domain.

2. Go to the **desktop**.

3. Start **Internet Explorer for the desktop** from the **Internet Explorer** taskbar button.

4. In **Internet Explorer**, click the **Tool** button (with the cog icon) in the top right corner and choose **Internet options**.

5. Click the **Advanced** tab and scroll down to the **Security** section.

6. Select the **Enable Enhanced Protected Mode*** check box, click **OK**, and then restart **CL01** for the settings to take effect.

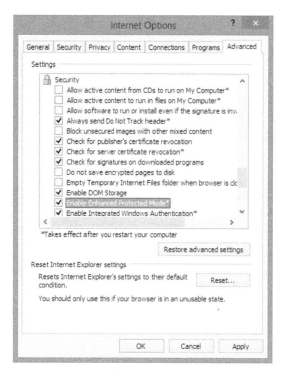

Enabling enhanced protected mode in Internet Explorer.

> **Note**: At this point in time, test all web applications, or have each application owner do the testing. When testing is done, you can deploy the setting using Internet Explorer settings in Group Policy preferences.

Windows Store

Windows 8 introduces a totally new framework for building apps that are touch-friendly and go along well in the new Windows 8 user interface.

Developers publish Windows 8 apps to the Windows Store, which houses thousands and thousands of apps. Typically, users go to the Windows Store to install these new and modern apps. At least that is the case for consumers.

Windows Store is the place where consumers typically get their apps.

In enterprise environments, you let your users be standard users rather than administrators, and one of the reasons is that they should not be able to install apps. Through Windows Store, your users are able to download any apps they like and install them even with standard user accounts, as more and more software is installed under the user profile instead of in the Program Files directory.

So you might just want to strangle the opportunities for your users to use the Windows Store.

Turn Off Access to the Windows Store

1. On **CL01**, log in as **Administrator** in the **VIAMONSTRA** domain.

2. On the **Start screen**, start **Edit group policy** to edit the local policy.

3. Expand the **Computer Configuration** / **Administrative Templates** / **Windows Components** / **Store** node. (This setting also can be set for the user in User Configuration.)

4. Open the setting **Turn off the Store application** and set it to **Enabled**.

Note: This policy also can be set as a domain policy, but it requires that you update the Group Policy templates in Windows Server 2012. This you learn in Chapter 7.

Windows 8 Apps in the Enterprise

Windows 8-style apps take applications to a whole new level. For some enterprises, the impact is minimal, but for others there are clear business cases around apps, primarily on slate types of devices.

Develop an App

Windows 8 contains a totally new framework called Windows Runtime. The new framework presents APIs that let developers continue using their favorite programming language, for example, HTML5, C#, C++, or JavaScript, for creating modern Windows 8 apps.

Windows 8 apps are compiled to an Appx package, which also has the file extension .appx. You cannot just install these types of apps as traditional applications as you learn below.

To be able to develop an app for Windows 8, you need the following:

* **Visual Studio 2012**. Visual Studio 2012 is the developer tool suite that in conjunction with the Windows Software Development Kit provides the foundation for developing Windows 8 apps. There are some templates and examples available, and you can start building Windows 8 apps using a number of programming languages.

* **Certificate**. All Windows 8 apps must be signed with a certificate where the publisher can be verified. For testing purposes, a self-signed certificate works fine.

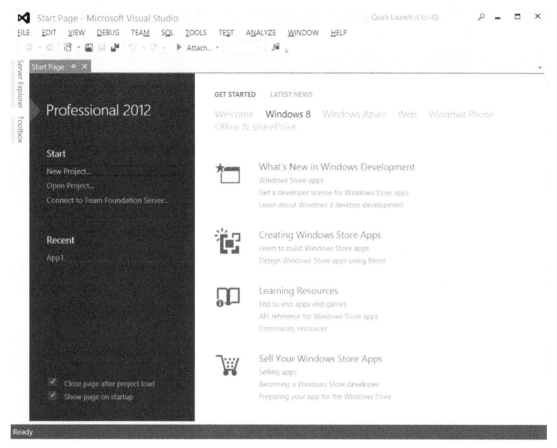

Ready-to-go samples in Visual Studio 2012 give you a kick start on developing a Windows 8 app.

Sideload Windows 8 Apps

If and when you convert your existing line-of-business applications or develop new ones to meet your business needs, you need to manage them on your Windows 8 devices. The thing is that when you have a custom-made Windows 8 app, you want to install it on your Windows 8 devices. In most cases, you want to accomplish this without first publishing it to the Windows Store and installing it from there, letting potentially millions of other users install that particular app.

So what you need is to be able to sideload Windows 8 apps and not publish and install them from the Windows Store.

Note: Sideloading a Windows 8 app is only possible in the Enterprise edition of Windows 8.

Set the Group Policy to Allow Sideloading

1. On **DC01**, log in as **Administrator** in the **VIAMONSTRA** domain.

2. Using the **Group Policy Management** console, edit the **Workstation Configuration** group policy.

3. In the **Computer Configuration / Policies / Administrative Templates / Windows Components / App Package Deployment** node, configure the following:

   Enable the **Allow all trusted apps to install** policy.

Sideload an App to Windows 8

This step adds an Appx (or modern-style app) to a Windows 8 machine and to the logged in user. This requires a compiled Appx package and a certificate which can be found in ViaMonstraAppx.iso, included in the books sample files.

1. On **CL01**, log on as **Don** in the **VIAMONSTRA** domain.

2. Mount the **ViaMonstraAppx.iso** file.

3. Using **File Explorer**, navigate to **D:** and double-click **App1_TemporaryKey**. This will start the **Certificate Import Wizard**.

4. On the **Welcome to the Certificate Import Wizard** page, select **Local Machine** and click **Next**.

5. In the **UAC** dialog box that appears, enter the following account information and then press **Enter**:

   a. Username: **VIAMONSTRA\Administrator**

   b. Password: **Pa$$w0rd**

6. On the **File to Import** page, accept the default settings and click **Next**.

7. On the **Private key protection** page, click **Next** without typing a password.

8. On the **Certificate Store** page, select the **Place all certificates in the following store** option and click **Browse**.

9. Select **Trusted Root Certification Authorities**, click **OK**, and then click **Next**.

10. On the **Completing the Certificate Import Wizard** page, click **Finish**.

11. Click **OK** when you see **The import was successful** message.

12. On the Start screen, start a **PowerShell command prompt**, and type the following command:

   Add-AppxPackage D:\ViaMonstra.appx

13. On the **Start screen**, verify that you now have a new app named **App1**.

In the upper right, you can find the tile for the Windows 8 app you just installed.

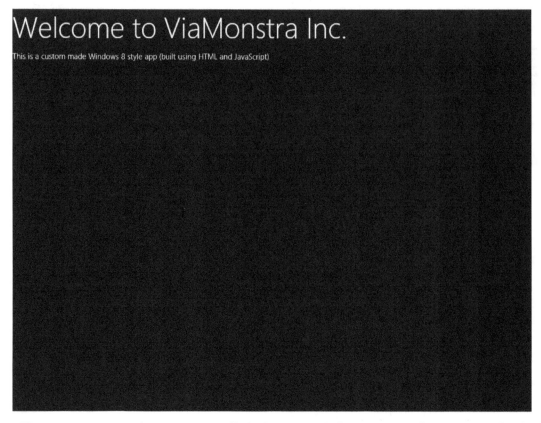

The custom app that you installed shown in full-screen mode, as are all Windows 8 apps.

How to Customize the Start Screen

The most common question I have received about Windows 8 is "how do I customize the Start screen for my users?" The answer has several answers, but there is this big "but." If your image has preinstalled (provisioned) app packages, these will show up on your users' Start screens regardless of how much you customize the Start screen and which method you use; Windows 8 apps that are provisioned to an image are installed at login time the first time a user logs in.

That means that if you do not completely remove the many unwanted Windows 8 apps from your image, you will be stuck with them, and you won't be able to customize the Start screen for your needs.

You can remove the apps from your image and customize it by following these steps, which are detailed in the following sections:

1. Mount the image and remove the Appx packages. This prevents them from being installed.

2. Set up the MDT 2012 Update 1 reference deployment share.

3. Build and capture the reference image.

4. Customize the Start screen to fit your enterprise's needs.

5. Save the reference image and make necessary configurations so that your settings will stick when you deploy your image to production machines.

Clean Out Provisioned Apps from the Image

These steps require that you have mounted a Windows 8 ISO to D: on DC01.

1. On **DC01**, log in as **Administrator** in the **VIAMONSTRA** domain.

2. Using **File Explorer**, create a new folder named **WIMSource** in the root of the **C:** drive and copy the **D:\sources\install.wim** file to **C:\WIMSource**.

3. Using **File Explorer**, create a new folder named **Mount** in the root of the **C:**.

4. Start an elevated **command prompt** (run as administrator) and type the following command:

> **Dism /Mount-Wim /WimFile:C:\WIMSource\install.wim /Index:1 /MountDir:C:\Mount**

5. Now you need to identify which Appx packages are already provisioned so that you know what to remove. This is achieved by running the following command:

> **Dism /Image:C:\Mount /Get-ProvisionedAppxPackages**

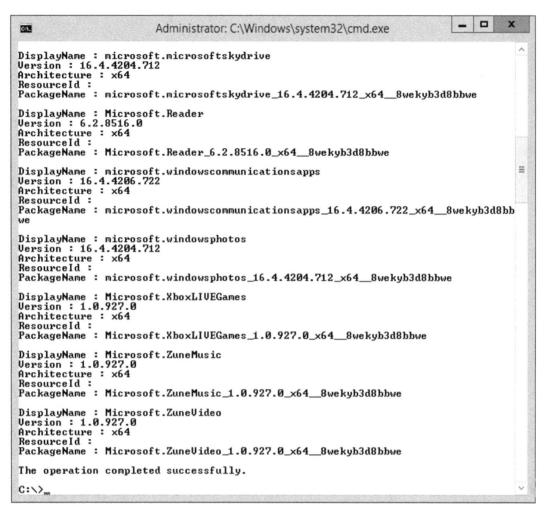

```
                Administrator: C:\Windows\system32\cmd.exe        —  □  x

DisplayName : microsoft.microsoftskydrive
Version : 16.4.4204.712
Architecture : x64
ResourceId :
PackageName : microsoft.microsoftskydrive_16.4.4204.712_x64__8wekyb3d8bbwe

DisplayName : Microsoft.Reader
Version : 6.2.8516.0
Architecture : x64
ResourceId :
PackageName : Microsoft.Reader_6.2.8516.0_x64__8wekyb3d8bbwe

DisplayName : microsoft.windowscommunicationsapps
Version : 16.4.4206.722
Architecture : x64
ResourceId :
PackageName : microsoft.windowscommunicationsapps_16.4.4206.722_x64__8wekyb3d8bb
we

DisplayName : microsoft.windowsphotos
Version : 16.4.4204.712
Architecture : x64
ResourceId :
PackageName : microsoft.windowsphotos_16.4.4204.712_x64__8wekyb3d8bbwe

DisplayName : Microsoft.XboxLIVEGames
Version : 1.0.927.0
Architecture : x64
ResourceId :
PackageName : Microsoft.XboxLIVEGames_1.0.927.0_x64__8wekyb3d8bbwe

DisplayName : Microsoft.ZuneMusic
Version : 1.0.927.0
Architecture : x64
ResourceId :
PackageName : Microsoft.ZuneMusic_1.0.927.0_x64__8wekyb3d8bbwe

DisplayName : Microsoft.ZuneVideo
Version : 1.0.927.0
Architecture : x64
ResourceId :
PackageName : Microsoft.ZuneVideo_1.0.927.0_x64__8wekyb3d8bbwe

The operation completed successfully.

C:\>_
```

All Appx packages in the image are listed, while the image is mounted offline or online.

6. Now that you know all the packages, you can start removing them one by one. For example, to remove the Finance app, you type the following command:

    Dism /Image:C:\Mount /Remove-ProvisionedAppxPackage /PackageName:Microsoft.BingFinance_1.2.0.135_x64__8wekyb3d8bbwe

7. When the remove is completed, close all **Explorer** windows (to close any open file handles to the C:\Mount folder), and type the following command to save the changes:

    Dism /Unmount-WIM /MountDir:C:\Mount /commit

8. Type **Exit** when done and press **Enter**.

> **Note**: You also can add your own apps to the image by using the Dism /Image:C:\Mount /Add-ProvisionedAppxPackage command.

Set Up the Reference Deployment Share

1. On **DC01**, log in as **Administrator** in the **VIAMONSTRA** domain.

2. On the **Start screen**, start **Deployment Workbench**.

3. In **Deployment Workbench**, right-click **Deployment Shares** and select **New Deployment Share**. Use the following settings for the **New Deployment Share Wizard**:

   a. On the **Path** page, in the **Deployment share path** text box, type C:\ReferenceShare, and then click **Next**.

   b. On the **Share** page, in the **Share name** text box, type **ReferenceShare$**, and then click **Next**.

   c. On the **Descriptive Name** page, in the **Deployment share description** text box, type **Reference Share**, and then click **Next**.

   d. On the **Options** page, accept the default settings and click **Next**.

   e. On the **Summary** page, click **Next**.

   f. On the **Confirmation** page, click **Finish**.

4. In **Deployment Workbench**, expand the **Reference Share** deployment share, right-click the **Operating Systems** node, and select **Import Operating System**. Complete the **Import Operating System Wizard** using the following settings:

   a. On the **OS Type** page, select the **Custom image file** option and click **Next**.

   b. On the **Image** page, in **Source file** text box, type **C:\WIMsource\install.wim**, and then click **Next**.

   c. On the **Setup** page, select the **Copy Windows Vista, Windows Server 2008, or later setup files from the specified path** option; then in the **Setup source directory** text box, type **C:\DeploymentShare\Operating Systems\Windows 8 Enterprise x64** and click **Next**.

> **Real World Note:** The setup files are needed if you want to install Windows components that are stored outside the custom operating system image, components like .NET Framework 3.5.1.

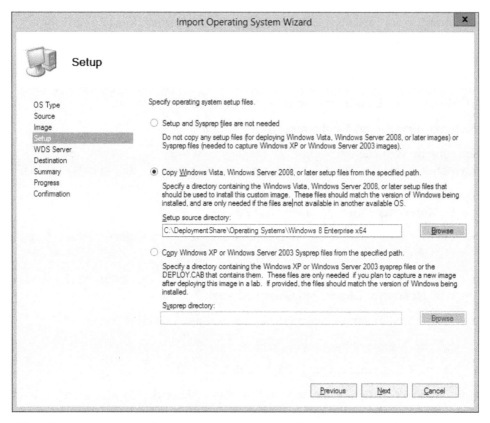

The Setup page in the Import Operating System Wizard.

    d. On the **Destination** page, in the **Destination directory name** text box, type **Reference image**, and then click **Next**.

    e. On the **Summary** page, click **Next**.

    f. On the **Confirmation** page, click **Finish**.

5.   After the import, in the **Operating Systems** node, right-click the newly added operating system, select **Rename**, and assign the following name:

       Windows 8 Enterprise x64 Reference image

6.   In **Deployment Workbench**, in the **Reference Share** node, right-click the **Task Sequences** node and select **New Task Sequence**. Use the following settings for the **New Task Sequence Wizard** and then click **Next**:

    a. On the **General Settings** page, in the **Task sequence ID** text box, type **REF-001**. In the **Task sequence name** text box, type **Windows 8 Reference Image** and click **Next**.

    b. On the **Select Template** page, accept the default settings and click **Next**.

   c.   On the **Select OS** page, select the **Windows 8 Enterprise x64 Reference image** operating system, and then click **Next**.

   d.   On the **Specify Product Key** page, accept the default settings and click **Next**.

   e.   On the **OS Settings** page, in the **Organization** text box, type **ViaMonstra Inc.** and click **Next**.

   f.   On the **Admin Password** page, select **Do not specify an Administrator password at this time**, and then click **Next**.

   g.   On the **Summary** page, click **Next**.

   h.   On the **Confirmation** page, click **Finish**.

7. In **Deployment Workbench**, select the **Task Sequences** node, right-click the **Windows 8 Reference Image** task sequence, and select **Properties.** Then click the **Task Sequence** tab.

8. In the task sequence, just below the **State Restore** group, select **Gather local only**. On the menu, select **Add**, select **General**, and then select **Run Command Line**.

9. Use the following settings for the new Run Command Line action:

   a.   Name: **Suspend**

   b.   Command Line: **cscript.exe %SCRIPTROOT%\LTISuspend.wsf**

   c.   Click **OK**.

10. Now edit the rules of the deployment share within **Deployment Workbench** by right-clicking the **Reference Share** deployment share, selecting **Properties**, and then clicking the **Rules** tab. Edit the rules (CustomSettings.ini) so that they look identical to the following content:

Note: You can also find a copy of the following CustomSettings.ini file in the book sample files.

```
[Settings]
Priority=Default

[Default]
OSInstall=Y
SkipAppsOnUpgrade=YES
SkipCapture=YES
DoCapture=YES
SkipAdminPassword=YES
SkipProductKey=YES
SkipUserData=YES
SkipTimeZone=YES
SkipFinalSummary=YES
SkipSummary=YES
SkipLocaleSelection=YES
SkipDomainMembership=YES
SkipComputerName=YES
SkipBitlocker=YES
SkipApplications=YES
ComputerBackupLocation=NETWORK
BackupShare=\\dc01\ReferenceShare$
BackupDir=Captures
BackupFile=%TaskSequenceID%.wim
```

11. Click the **Edit Bootstrap.ini** button and modify the contents to look like the following content:

Note: There is also a copy of the following Bootstrap.ini in the book sample files.

```
[Settings]
Priority=Default

[Default]
SkipBDDWelcome=YES
DeployRoot=\\dc01\ReferenceShare$
UserDomain=viamonstra.com
UserID=administrator
UserPassword=Pa$$w0rd
```

12. Save the **Bootstrap.ini** file, and click **OK**.

13. Update the deployment share to get the boot WIM that you use to boot your virtual machine, and then start the build process by right-clicking the **Reference Share** deployment share and selecting **Update Deployment Share**.

14. Use the following settings for the **Update Deployment Share Wizard**:

   a.   On the **Options** page, accept the default settings and click **Next**.

   b.   On the **Summary** page, click **Next**.

   c.   On the **Confirmation** page, click **Finish**.

15. In the **Windows Deployment Services** console, right-click **Boot images** and select **Add Boot Image**. Use the following settings for the **Add Image Wizard**:

   a.   On the **Image File** page, in the **File location** text box, type **C:\ReferenceShare\Boot\LiteTouchPE_x64.wim**, and then click **Next**.

   b.   On the **Image Metadata** page, in the **Image name** and **Image description** text boxes, type **Reference Image**, and then click **Next**.

The Image Metadata page·

   c.   On the **Summary** page, click **Next**.

   d.   On the **Task Progress** page, click **Finish**.

Build and Capture the Reference Image

1. Start the **CL02** virtual machine, and do a PXE boot by pressing **F12** during boot.

2. In the **Windows Boot Manager** menu, select the **Reference Image** boot image and press **Enter**. Wait for WinPE to load and initiate the deployment tools.

3. In the **Windows Deployment Wizard**, select the **Windows 8 Reference Image** task sequence and click **Next** to initiate the reference image build process. This will take some time to finish.

Note: When the machine has been installed, it will be logged in to the Administrator account. This is the Suspend action that you added in the task sequence (the LTISuspend.wsf script makes this happen) so that you have the chance to customize the Start screen. When the customizations are complete, you resume the image build process by clicking the Resume Task Sequence shortcut on the desktop.

---

4. At the **Start screen**, customize the Start screen according to your needs.

5. When the customizations are completed, click the **Desktop** tile; then on the **desktop**, double-click the **Resume Task Sequence** shortcut to finish the build process and create the new WIM image.

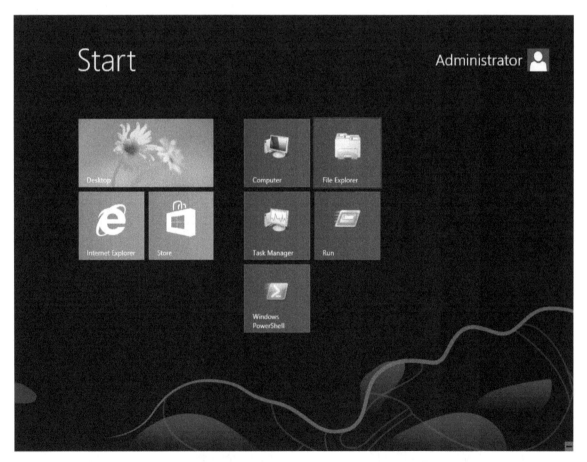

While building the reference image, you can customize the Start screen for all users who log in to the machines deployed with this particular image.

Real World Note: When creating reference images in the real world, you probably want them to be patched automatically, as well, by getting updates from your WSUS server. This can be achieved by activating the Windows Update steps in the task sequence and by adding the following line to the rules (CustomSettings.ini):

WSUSServer=http://wsusservername

Prepare the Deployment Environment to Account for Customizations

1. On **DC01**, log in as **Administrator** in the **VIAMONSTRA** domain.

2. On the **Start screen**, select **Deployment Workbench**.

3. In the **MDT Deployment Share** deployment share (which you created in Chapter 1), right-click the **Operating Systems** node and select **Import Operating System.**

4. Use the following settings for the **Import Operating System Wizard**:

   a. On the **OS Type** page, select the **Custom image file** option and click **Next**.

   b. On the **Image** page, in the **Source file** text box, type **C:\ReferenceShare\Captures\REF-001.wim**. Select the **Move the files to the deployment share instead of copying them** check box, and then click **Next**.

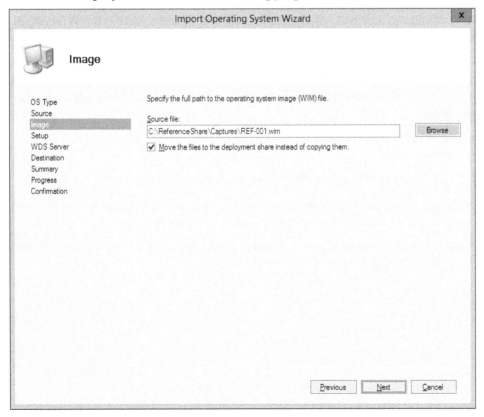

The Image page in the Import Operating System Wizard.

    c. On the **Setup** page, select the **Copy Windows Vista, Windows Server 2008, or later setup files from the specified path** option; then in the **Setup source directory** text box, type **C:\DeploymentShare\Operating Systems\Windows 8 Enterprise x64**, and then click **Next**.

    d. On the **Destination** page, in the **Destination directory name** text box, type **Windows 8 Custom Image**, and then click **Next**.

    d. On the **Summary** page, click **Next**.

    e. On the **Confirmation** page, click **Finish**.

5. After the import, in the **Operating Systems** node, right-click the newly added operating system, select **Rename**, and assign the following name:

    Windows 8 Enterprise x64 Custom image

6. In the **MDT Deployment Share**, select the **Task Sequences** node, right-click the **Windows 8 Enterprise x64** task sequence, and select **Properties**. Then click the **Task Sequence** tab.

7. Expand the **Install** node, click **Install Operating System**, and change the OS image to the new reference image by clicking the **Browse** button and selecting the **Windows 8 Enterprise x64 Custom image** operating system. Then click **Apply**.

8. In the **OS Info** tab, click **Edit Unattend.xml**. Wait for the image catalog to be generated, which will take several minutes. When finished, the **Windows System Image Manager** starts with the **Unattend.xml** file open for editing. Configure the **Unattend.xml** using the following settings:

    a. In **Windows System Image Manager**, in the **Answer File** section, expand **4 Specialize**.

    b. Click **amd64_Microsoft-Windows-Shell-Setup_neutral**.

    c. In the right pane, click **CopyProfile**. Then, in the drop-down list that appears, click the arrow and select **true**.

    d. In the **File** menu, select **Save Answer File** and then close the **Windows System Image Manager**.

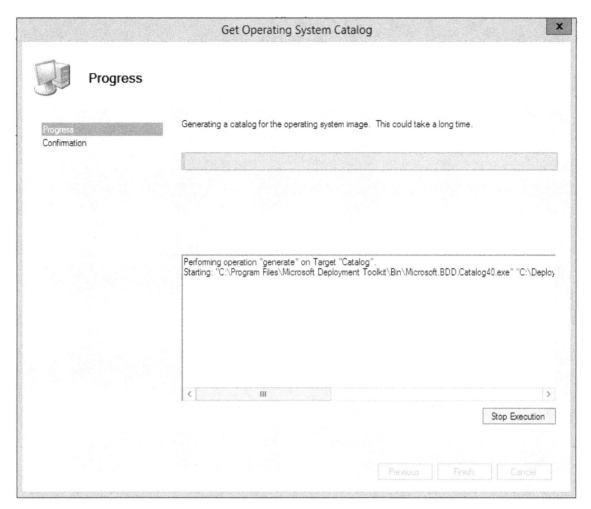

The catalog generation will take several minutes to finish.

Deploy the Customized Operating System Image

1. Restart **CL02**, and do a PXE boot to the network by **pressing F12**.

2. In the **Windows Boot Manager** menu, select the **Lite Touch Windows PE (x64)** boot image, and press **Enter**. Wait for WinPE to load and initiate the deployment tools.

3. In the **Windows Deployment Wizard**, select the **Windows 8 Enterprise x64** task sequence and click **Next** to initiate the reference image build process. This will take some time to finish.

4. When the installation is done, log in as **Don** in the **VIAMONSTRA** domain, and note that the **Start screen** is the exact way you customized it in the reference image.

After logging in as Don, you see that the Start screen is exactly as you customized it when creating the reference image.

Chapter 3

User Data and Profiles

User profiles and data always have and always will be sensitive issues. They are simply important. For the first time in many years, you now have some really nice improvements to what you can do with user profiles and data. How you can alleviate this to create a fantastic user experience is what you learn in this chapter. The addition of User Experience Virtualization (UE-V) takes setting roaming to a whole new level. Along with primary devices for roaming user profiles and folder redirection, user data and profile handling has never been better.

Roaming User Profiles

Roaming user profiles are not widely used, from my experience, and there are not any fundamental changes to how roaming user profiles work in Windows 8. Roaming user profiles are still loaded at login time and saved when logging out. Still, they can be used along with the new setting for primary devices, which is discussed in "Primary Devices" later in this chapter.

If you are using roaming user profiles and Windows XP, you must be aware that moving to Windows 8 will create totally new roaming user profiles for your users. The new profiles will be appended with ".v2". Because of the many changes of user profile paths and many other significant changes from Windows XP to Windows Vista and later operating systems, it would be impossible to guarantee a good user experience if the user profiles were kept.

Background Synchronization

The main problem that arises with roaming user profiles is that changes occur over time that are not captured because users tend to let laptops go to sleep or hibernate instead of shutting them down. This is a big problem because the roaming user profile is saved only when the user logs off or restarts or shuts down a machine.

In Windows 7, there was a change introduced that let you save the registry to the user profile on the network as often as every hour. This in practice mean that you are guaranteed to get many settings and changes replicated to the network profile location even if the user doesn't log off or shut down. Still, in practice, roaming user profiles are not that good and many times cause a negative user experience, mostly due to the long time it takes to roam the profiles, the issue with consistency of user and application settings, and profiles' tendency to be corrupted over time.

Set the Background Synchronization Settings

ViaMonstra Inc. does not use roaming user profiles, but if you do I strongly suggest activating background synchronization of the registry.

1. On **DC01**, log in as **Administrator** in the **VIAMONSTRA** domain.

2. Using the **Group Policy Management** console, edit the **Workstation Configuration** group policy.

3. In the **Computer Configuration** / **Policies** / **Administrative Templates** / **System** / **User Profiles** node, configure the following:

> Enable the **Set the schedule for background upload of a roaming user profile's registry file while user is logged on** policy, and then configure the **Scheduling method** to **Run at set interval** and the **Interval hour(s)** to **1**.

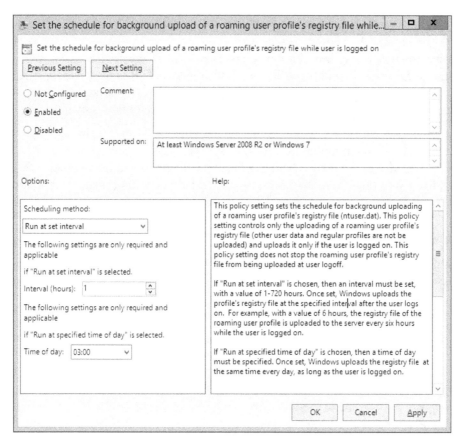

The Set the schedule for background upload of a roaming user profile's registry file while user is logged on group policy.

Setting the Roaming User Profile Path

You have two options for setting the roaming user profile path. The most common way to set it is to use the "profile" attribute on the user account in Active Directory. As of Windows Vista, you also can set the profile path using a Group Policy setting.

Real World Note: If you want to apply roaming user profiles only on some machines, you can use the options to set the profile path via group policies instead of via the user account attributes in Active Directory. This means that if the user, for instance, logs in to a common machine, such as a conference machine, the user profile will not be loaded, providing a much quicker login experience.

Set the User Profile Path via Group Policies

1. On **DC01**, log in as **Administrator** in the **VIAMONSTRA** domain.

2. Using the **Group Policy Management** console, edit the **Workstation Configuration** group policy.

3. In the **Computer Configuration** / **Policies** / **Administrative Templates** / **System** / **User Profiles** node, configure the following settings:

   > Enable the **Set roaming profile path for all users logging onto this computer** policy and configure the path where you want to store the roaming user profiles.

Folder Redirection

Folder Redirection is a really beautiful thing. I implement it in all my deployment projects if it is not already in place. What is so beautiful is that you redirect your documents, the desktop, favorites from Internet Explorer, and more to a network drive, which means you can always log in to another machine and get the same data and settings.

Offline Files

When you activate Folder Redirection, it by default enables Offline Files. This adds the benefit of keeping all those redirected files available offline when a user is not connected to the file server resource on the internal network, which is perfect for your mobile users. They always have the data they need, and changes are synchronized when a connection to the file server is restored, either through a remote access connection or when on the internal network.

If you have used, as I have, Folder Redirection with Offline Files in Windows XP, you will see extreme changes in how it works in Windows 8. It's seamless for the user in all scenarios, and the synchronization is done in the background rather than at logoff time as is the case in Windows XP.

Note: Actually, Offline Files was totally rewritten for Windows Vista; the feature was improved further in Windows 7 and received additional improvements in Windows 8.

Always Offline Mode

For ViaMonstra Inc., and those of you running Windows 7 and Folder Redirection, there are not many changes with Windows 8. One major difference, however, is Always Offline mode, which makes you run in offline mode even when you are online to get improved performance when working with cached files. The synchronization of files back to the server is then performed at an interval of every two hours or by a value that you configure.

Setting Up Folder Redirection with Offline Files

Configuring Folder Redirection is done in two steps: making sure there is a file share available to house the folder structure and data, and performing a group policy configuration. I also add a third step to configure Always Offline mode and a couple of other settings for Offline Files.

Create the Folder Structure on the File Server

1. On **DC01**, log in as **Administrator** in the **VIAMONSTRA** domain.

2. Using **File Explorer**, create a folder named **Shares** in the root of the **C:** drive.

3. In the **Shares** folder, create a new folder named **UserData**. Right-click the **UserData** folder and select **Properties / Security / Advanced**.

4. Click the **Disable inheritance** button, and in the **Block Inheritance** dialog box, select **Remove all inherited permissions from this object**.

5. Click **Add** and then click the **Select a principal** link. In the **Enter the object name to select** input area, type **SYSTEM** and click **OK**. Enter the following permissions for **SYSTEM** and then click **OK**:

   a. Applies to: **This folder subfolders and files**

   b. Basic permissions: **Full control**

6. Repeat step 5 to set the permissions for **Administrators**, **CREATOR OWNER**, and **Authenticated Users**:

   a. Administrators: **Full control** in **This folder, subfolders and files**

   b. CREATOR OWNER: **Full control** in **Subfolder and files only**

   c. Authenticated Users: **This folder only**:

      ▪ **Traverse folder / execute file**

      ▪ **List folder / read data**

      ▪ **Read attributes**

      ▪ **Read extended attributes**

      ▪ **Create folders / append data**

Note: When editing special permissions, you must click the **Show advanced permissions** link in the **Permission Entry for UserData** window to be able to set the preceding special permissions.

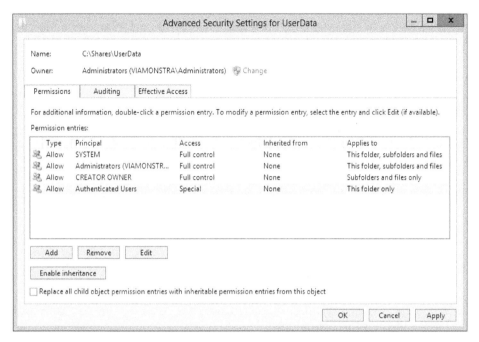

This is what the ACL list should look like when you are done editing it.

7.   When you are done, click **OK**.

8.   Without closing the **UserData Properties** window, in the **Sharing** tab, select **Advanced Sharing**.

9.   Select the **Share this folder** check box and click the **Permissions** button.

10. Remove **Everyone** and add the **Authenticated Users** group with **Full control**. Click **OK** three times.

Configure the Group Policy Object

1.   On **DC01**, log in as **Administrator** in the **VIAMONSTRA** domain.

2.   Using the **Group Policy Management** console, right-click the **User Accounts** OU, and select **Create a GPO in this domain, and Link it here**.

3.   Assign the name **User Configuration** to the new group policy.

4.   Expand the **User Accounts** OU, right-click the **User Configuration** group policy, and select **Edit**.

5.   In the **User Configuration** / **Policies** / **Windows Settings** / **Folder Redirection** node, right-click **Desktop** and select **Properties**.

6. In the **Setting** drop-down list, select **Basic – Redirect everyone's folder to the same location**.

7. In the **Root path** text field, enter **\\dc01\userdata**. In the **Settings** tab, clear the **Grant the user exclusive rights to Desktop** check box and click **OK**. In the **Warning** dialog box that appears, click **Yes**.

Note: The default options will set the owner of the files to the user. That means you as the administrator will not be able to access the files without changing the owner and replacing the ACLs. In some cases this is wanted, whereas in others it is not. In particular, when you do not want administrators to access the contents of the user folders, you should use the default setting.

Verify That Folder Redirection Is in Effect

1. On **CL01**, log in as **Don** in the **VIAMONSTRA** domain and complete the following steps:

   a. Click the **Desktop** tile on the **Start screen** to go to the desktop.

   b. Right-click the desktop and select **New**, **Text Document**.

   c. As the file name, enter **CL01.txt**.

   d. Open the text file with **Notepad** and enter the text **This was created on CL01**; save the file and close **Notepad**.

   e. Log off **CL01**, and on **DC01**, verify that the **CL01.txt** file is in the **C:\Shares\UserData\Don\Desktop** folder. If not, log on **CL01** and log off one more time to make sure the policy is in effect.

2. On **CL02**, log in as **Don** in the **VIAMONSTRA** domain and perform the following step:

   Verify that the text file **CL01.txt** exists on the desktop and that the contents of the file match the text you entered in the file on **CL01**.

Real World Note: If you redirect your folders to a Distributed File System (DFS) path, Windows Search does not honor this type of link. That means it will not be able to index your folders if you are not using Offline Files (for instance, on stationary machines). The same behavior existed in Windows 7 and has not been fixed for Windows Search in Windows 8.

Configure Always Offline Mode for Offline Files

1. On **DC01**, log in as **Administrator** in the **VIAMONSTRA** domain.

2. Using the **Group Policy Management** console, edit the **Workstation Configuration** group policy.

3. In the **Computer Configuration / Policies / Administrative Templates / Network / Offline Files** node, configure the following:

   a. Enable the **Configure slow-link mode** policy, and in the **Options** box, click the **Show** button.

   b. In the **Show Contents** dialog box that appears, enter * as the **Value name** and **Latency=1** as the **Value**.

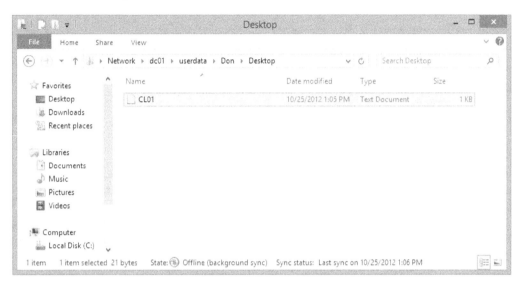

Note in the status bar that Offline Files is offline in background sync mode.

Controlling Synchronization on Metered Networks

One of the new features in Windows 8 is the support for metered networks, specifically networks that typically have a cost associated with them. The default is that Windows 8 will not synchronize data when roaming. When it comes to Offline Files, you want to have complete control over the synchronization so that it occurs in some cases regardless of network connection. Not everyone will use this capability, but ViaMonstra Inc. values its data and therefore wants synchronization activated to avoid possible data loss.

Configure Synchronization on Metered Networks

1. On **DC01**, log in as **Administrator** in the **VIAMONSTRA** domain.

2. Using the **Group Policy Management** console, edit the **Workstation Configuration** group policy.

3. In the **Computer Configuration / Policies / Administrative Templates / Network / Offline Files** node, configure the following:

   Enable the **Enable file synchronization on costed networks** policy.

Primary Devices

Windows 8 introduces a new *primary device* feature. Regardless of whether you are using folder redirection or roaming user profiles, you can benefit from this new feature when it comes to profiles and data. That is, you can define a primary computer for any given user. Doing this in combination with setting a certain GPO setting ensures that a roaming user profile and/or folder redirection is applied only on the user's primary device and not when the user logs on to any other device.

> **Real World Note**: To be able to use primary devices, you must extend the Active Directory schema to a Windows Server 2012 schema. This does not mean you need to introduce Windows Server 2012 domain controllers in your environment, but you need to take the adprep utility from the Windows Server 2012 installation media (located in the support/adprep directory) and run that command from any domain member in the domain.

Set a User's Primary Device

It would be a real understatement that setting a primary device for a user is user-friendly as it involves editing the attributes right at the heart of Active Directory. You need to enter the common name of the computer object into a specific user attribute, using either ADSI Edit or the Attribute Editor integrated in the Active Directory Users and Computers snap-in, and also set the necessary Group Policy setting.

Set the Primary Device for a User in Active Directory

1. On **DC01**, log in as **Administrator** in the **VIAMONSTRA** domain.

2. Using **Active Directory Users and Computers**, in the **View** menu, select **Advanced Features** to enable the advanced features that you need in order to edit the attribute for a primary computer.

3. In the **Workstations** OU, right-click **CL01** and select **Properties**.

4. In the **Attribute Editor** tab, click **Filter**, and then select **Show only attributes that have values**.

5. In the **Attributes** list, select **distinguishedName** and click the **View** button.

6. Right-click the line **CN=CL01,OU=Workstations,DC=viamonstra,DC=com** and select **Copy**. Then click **Cancel** two times.

7. In the **User Accounts** OU, right-click **John** and select **Properties**.

8. In the **Attribute Editor** tab, click **Filter**, and then select **Show only attributes that have values** once again to clear the selection.

9. In the **Attributes** list, scroll down until you find **msDS-PrimaryComputer**.

10. Mark **msDS-PrimaryComputer** and click the **Edit** button.

> **Note**: You cannot just enter a computer name here, which is why you fetched the Active Directory distinguished name for the computer that you want to set as the primary computer.

11. In the **Value to add** field, right-click and select **Paste**. Click **Add**, and then click **OK** two times.

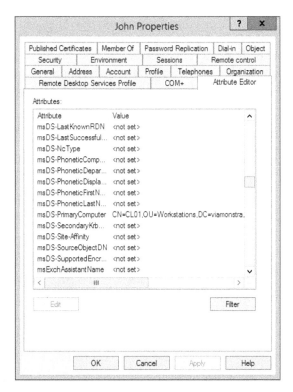

The John account with primary device (computer) configured.

Configure the Necessary Group Policy Object

In these steps, you configure the primary device for folder redirection, but you also can activate this for roaming user profiles.

1. On **DC01**, log in as **Administrator** in the **VIAMONSTRA** domain.

2. Using the **Group Policy Management** console, edit the **Workstation Configuration** group policy.

3. In the **Computer Configuration** / **Policies** / **Administrative Templates** / **System** / **Folder Redirection** node, configure the following:

> Enable the **Redirect folders on primary computers only** policy.

Verify That the Primary Device Is Set as Intended

1. On **CL01**, log in as **John** in the **VIAMONSTRA** domain.

2. Using **File Explorer**, verify that folder redirection is taking place by right-clicking the **Desktop** folder and selecting **Properties**. The Target text box should display the following:

    \\dc01\userdata\John\Desktop.

3. On the **Start screen**, select **View event logs**. In the **Event Viewer**, navigate to the **Applications and Services Logs / Microsoft / Windows / Folder Redirection / Operational** node and look for events with Event ID: **1010**. The event should state that CL01 is a primary computer for John.

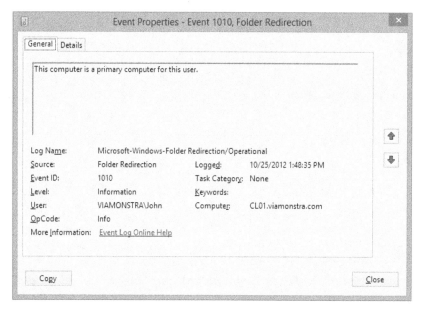

Event confirming that CL01 is a primary computer for John.

4. On **CL02**, log in as **John** in the **VIAMONSTRA** domain.

5. Using **File Explorer**, verify that folder redirection is not taking place by right-clicking the **Desktop** folder and selecting **Properties**. The **Target** text box should display the following:

    C:\Users\John\Desktop.

6. On the **Start screen**, select **View event logs**. In the **Event Viewer**, navigate to the **Applications and Services Logs / Microsoft / Windows / Folder Redirection / Operational** node and look for events with Event ID: **1010**. The event should state that CL02 is not a primary computer for John.

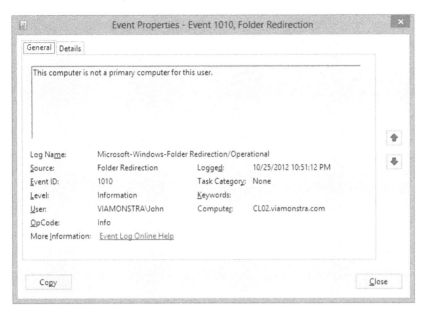

Event displaying that CL02 is not a primary computer for John.

User Experience Virtualization (UE-V)

With UE-V, Microsoft introduces what I would call a light version of roaming user profiles. It solves all challenges related to roaming user profiles and enables you to roam settings for Windows and Office and whatever other settings you define for your environment and applications.

Note: User Experience Virtualization is included in Microsoft Desktop Optimization Pack (MDOP) 2012. MDOP is available only to those with this addition to their volume license agreements.

Basics

UE-V basically saves settings in the shape of files or registry settings for Windows and applications and saves them in a network location such as the user's home directory or a directory which you designate. So when users log in on another computer, the settings are read from the network share and applied to their user profiles and applications.

So what you need is:

- **Agent**. To be able to do this, you install an agent that needs to be run on each machine that will roam settings. The default setup is also dependent on Offline Files to make sure that the settings are always available, but this can be turned off if you want.

- **Templates**. The template files describe which settings are roamed.

- **Triggers**. There are various triggers which decide when the roaming takes place, for instance, when an application starts and closes.

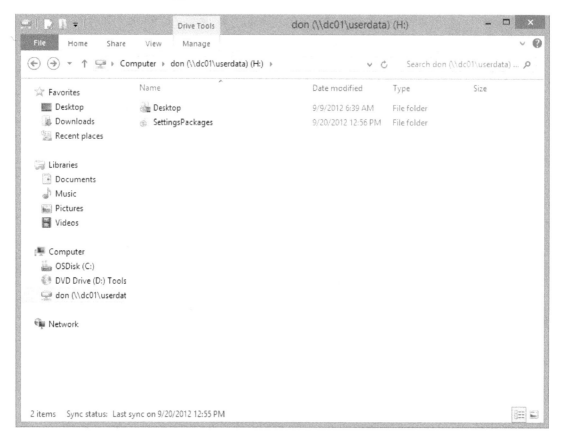

The UE-V settings are stored in a hidden folder named SettingsPackages in the home directory.

Templates

Which settings will be saved and roamed between the machines is determined by templates in XML format. Predefined templates are shipped with UE-V for roaming settings for:

- Windows 7 and Windows 8, or Windows 7 and Windows Server 2008 R2, or Windows 8 and Windows Server 2012
    - Windows Accessories (Notepad, WordPad, and Calculator)
    - Desktop background and theme settings
    - Start menu and taskbar settings, folder options, and more user settings.
- Internet Explorer 8, 9, and 10 settings, including Favorites.
- All Office 2010 applications

- Lync client

Real World Note: Those of you familiar with USMT (User State Migration Tool) will be familiar with the templates. Although the XML templates for USMT and UE-V differ, the principle is the same.

Generating Your Own Templates

You can easily create your own templates to roam particular settings in Windows or an application. Shipped with UE-V is the UE-V Template Generator which will guide you through the process of creating your very own templates.

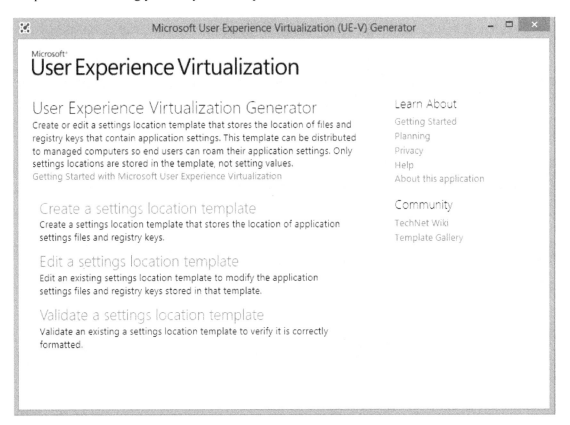

Generate your own templates with the UE-V Generator.

Microsoft also provides a gallery where others can publish templates that you can use instead of reinventing the wheel. Look at http://go.microsoft.com/fwlink/?LinkID=246589.

Triggers

Unlike roaming user profiles that are read and saved at logon and logoff, UE-V uses various triggers to determine when settings are roamed.

- **Application start and close**. When a user closes Word, for instance, the settings for Word are saved to the designated network share. When the user opens Word the next time or on another machine, the settings from the network share are read and applied to the application as it starts.

- **Locking a machine**. When a user locks a machine, Windows settings are saved to the network location.

- **Logon or logoff**. Some settings, such as region and language, Start screen and taskbar settings, are saved and applied only at logon and logoff.

Setting Up UE-V

You will learn how to set up UE-V from start to finish. Please note that to complete this lab, you do need access to the MDOP package which is not freely available.

Note: MDOP can be found and evaluated on Microsoft TechNet for anyone having a subscription to the TechNet network.

Prepare a User Account

1. On **DC01**, log in as **Administrator** in the **VIAMONSTRA** domain.

2. Using **Active Directory Users and Computers**, in the **User Accounts** OU, right-click **Don** and select **Properties**.

3. In the **Profile** tab, in the **Home folder** area, select **Connect** and then select **H:**; in the **To** text box, type \\dc01\userdata\don and click **OK**. In the **Active Directory Domain Services** warning dialog box, click **Yes**.

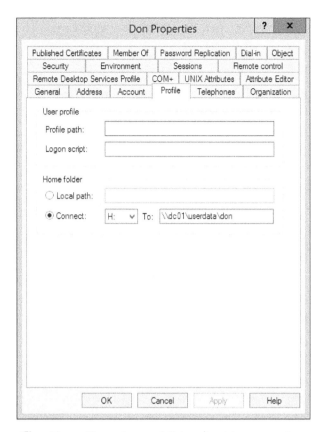

The User Experience Virtualization agent uses the home folder information by default.

Install the Agent on CL01 and CL02

Note that if you do not have access to MDOP, you will not have the necessary tools to proceed with this guide.

1. On **CL01**, log in as **Administrator** in the **VIAMONSTRA** domain.

2. Mount the **Tools.iso** (located in the C:\ISO folder).

3. Using **File Explorer**, navigate to the **D:\User Experience Virtualization** folder, and start the **Microsoft User Experience Virtualization Agent** setup (**AgentSetup.exe**).

4. On the **Welcome to the Microsoft User Experience Virtualization Agent Setup Wizard** page, click **Next**.

5. On the **End-User License Agreement** page, accept the license agreement and click **Next**.

6. On the **Customer Experience Improvement Program** page, select **I do not want to join the program at this time** and click **Next**.

7. On the **Destination Folder** page, accept the default settings and click **Next**.

8. On the **Ready to Install Microsoft User Experience Virtualization Agent** page, click **Install**.

9. When the installation is complete, click **Finish** and then click **Restart**.

10. On **CL02**, repeat the preceding steps to install the **Microsoft User Experience Virtualization Agent** on that machine, as well.

Note: By default, the agent will look in Active Directory to see whether the user has a home share set. If there is a home share designated, it will be used; otherwise, you need to specify another location to which to save the settings packages.

Verify the Setup

1. On **CL01**, log in as **Don** in the **VIAMONSTRA** domain.

2. Go to the **Start screen**, and search for and open **Notepad**.

3. Go to **Format** and click **Font**.

4. Set the font to **Wingdings**, click **OK**, and close Notepad

5. On **CL02**, log in as **Don** in the **VIAMONSTRA** domain.

6. Open **Notepad** and verify that the font is set to **Wingdings**, which I can tell you is not the default font in any Notepad on any machine. ☺

Microsoft Account Connections

Windows 8 by default offers the possibility of using a Microsoft account (previously known, for instance, as a Hotmail or Live account) to log in to Windows 8. That in theory means that some settings will roam with the user to other machines the user logs in to.

The thing to note in an enterprise environment is that by default any domain user who logs on to a domain-joined Windows 8 machine can set up a connection to their Microsoft account.

A few concerns here might be that sensitive information could leave the enterprise, posing a security risk, or that the user roams settings from their home machines to their work PCs. In some scenarios, it is not a concern; on the contrary, it might be a good thing to keep everything synchronized. It all depends on your requirements on security and your demands for user experience.

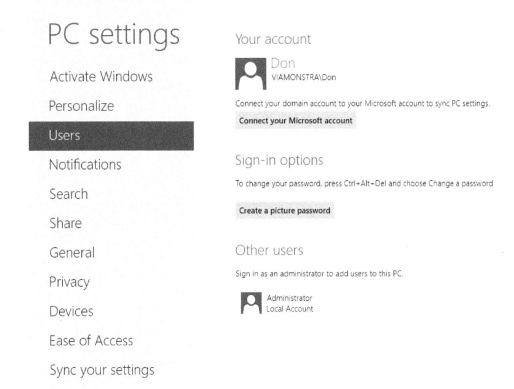

By default in Windows 8, any domain user can connect their account to a Microsoft account.

Turn Off the Possibility of Linking a Domain Account to a Microsoft Account

1. On **DC01**, log in as **Administrator** in the **VIAMONSTRA** domain.

2. Using the **Group Policy Management** console, edit the **Workstation Configuration** group policy.

3. In the **Computer Configuration** / **Polices** / **Windows Settings** / **Security Settings** / **Local Policies** / **Security Options** node, configure the following:

    Configure the **Accounts: Block Microsoft accounts** policy with the **Users can't add or log on with Microsoft accounts** setting.

Turn Off the Synchronization of Certain Settings

If you do want to allow Microsoft accounts, you can control what group of settings you want to synchronize to the Microsoft cloud, or turn off sync altogether.

1. On **DC01**, log in as **Administrator** in the **VIAMONSTRA** domain.

2. Using the **Group Policy Management** console, edit the **Workstation Configuration** group policy.

3. In the **Computer Configuration** / **Policies** / **Administrative Templates** / **Windows components** / **Sync your settings** node, change the Group Policy settings of your choice.

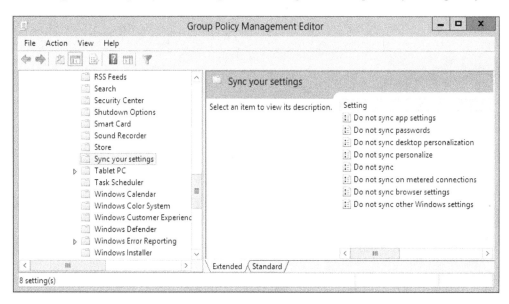

The available Sync your settings policies·

Chapter 4

Security

Security in Windows 8 builds off the improved security that was introduced in Windows Vista and Windows 7. In Windows 8, many challenges around some of the security features are solved. In this chapter, you learn all about the essential security features and other improvements for AppLocker and BitLocker. This chapter also focuses on new security features such as virtual smart cards, Trusted Boot, Measured Boot, and early launch anti-malware.

BitLocker

BitLocker is the full-volume encryption for disks, and it is without a doubt the most popular and most used security feature in Windows 7. When using BitLocker in Windows 7, there are some challenges, but you will be glad to hear that Windows 8 solves them all. The top three most common issues with BitLocker in Windows 7 are encryption speed and two PIN code challenges.

The Lock icon on a drive indicates BitLocker is being used on that drive.

Only Encrypting Actual Data

One of the biggest drawbacks of the BitLocker implementation in previous Windows versions is that it may take several hours to encrypt a disk with BitLocker, as the entire disk (or partition) is encrypted regardless of the amount of data. In Windows 8, a new feature called "Used space only" is introduced. It means that instead of encrypting an entire drive or partition, it encrypts only actual data and then encrypts additional data as it is written to the drive. I must add that performance overhead is not noticed whatsoever.

You can still do full-volume encryption, encrypting the entire drive or partition as in previous Windows versions, but the fact that encrypting only data does not noticeably impact performance means that you can gain a lot of time.

> **Note**: You can restart a machine before it has fully encrypted the drive. To see the actual progress then, you can start fvenotify.exe to start the taskbar application which indicates whether BitLocker drive encryption is in progress.

Alternatives for Using BitLocker in Windows 8

BitLocker in Windows 8 provides three modes for using BitLocker that were available with Windows 7 and adds two new ones. The old ones include TPM, TPM+PIN, and USB key. Using only a USB key is something I strongly recommend against, as it keeps the unlock key on a USB key drive that would always be stored with the machine. That is the equivalent of locking a door and leaving the key in the lock.

Currently, all implementations of BitLocker in any serious enterprise are done by storing the unlock key in a TPM chip, which requires hardware that has a TPM chip. The other option is to store the unlock key in the TPM chip and protect it with a PIN code. In practice, this means that the user has to enter a PIN code to be able to start a machine.

The following combinations are recommended for use with BitLocker in Windows 8:

- **TPM only**. Only a TPM chip is used to house the BitLocker keys. This solution is transparent to the user and a little less secure.

- **TPM + PIN**. TPM used in conjunction with a PIN code. More secure, but it means that a user needs to remember and enter the PIN code before booting. Remote management cannot be performed.

- **Password**. A new protector that can be used for hardware that does not have a TPM chip. The user simply needs to enter a password when booting the machine.

- **TPM + Network unlock (+fall back to PIN)**. The TPM is used in conjunction with network unlock when on the internal network. When outside of the corporate network, it falls back to a PIN code.

Password Protector

Until Windows 8, there was only a really bad way to use BitLocker unless you had a TPM chip, and that was to use the option of having the unlock key stored in a USB memory device. In practice, this means that to boot your machine you need to have the USB key inserted in the machine.

There is one big problem with this. What happens, for instance, if your laptop bag gets stolen? Where is the USB key to unlock the machine stored? Probably it's stored in the bag along with the machine. From a security standpoint, this is really bad.

So, in Windows 8, you have the option to use a password to unlock machines that lack a TPM chip. The password can be configured to allow for complexity and length via group policies.

The password protector for BitLocker is brand new in Windows 8.

Network Protector

The network protector for BitLocker is totally new and is called Network Unlock. Basically, this means that when booting, you verify, using PXE, to a Windows Deployment Services server that your machine is okay to boot, and it is then unlocked automatically. That is, it is if you are physically connected to your company network. If the machine is moved out of the office, or if the PXE service is not available, you can have it configured so that the user uses a PIN code to unlock the machine when booting it.

This effectively solves the problem with remote or nightly management of machines which have a PIN code requirement, as everything will work transparently while the machine is on the internal network.

PIN Code Change for Standard Users

As mentioned in the preceding section, remote and nightly management of machines previously was one challenge in enterprises when using BitLocker with a PIN code. Another problem was that standard users could not change the PIN code. This problem is solved with BitLocker in Windows 8 if you choose to use it with a PIN code.

> **Note**: Using BitLocker with a PIN code is more secure than using it only with a TPM configuration.

How to Activate BitLocker

To activate BitLocker, you need to configure some necessary Group Policy settings first. To activate BitLocker for use with the new password protector key, you need to change a couple of more Group Policy settings.

Set the Group Policies for Using BitLocker with the Password Protector

1. On **DC01**, log in as **Administrator** in the **VIAMONSTRA** domain.

2. Using the **Group Policy Management** console, edit the **Workstation Configuration** group policy.

3. In the **Computer Configuration / Polices / Administrative Templates / Windows Components / BitLocker Drive Encryption / Operating System Drives** node, configure the following:

    a. Enable the **Configure use of hardware-based encryption for operating system drives** policy.

    b. Enable the **Configure the use of password operating system drives** policy and configure the following:

       > In **Configure password complexity for operating system drives**, select **Require password complexity**.

    c. Enable the **Require additional authentication at startup** policy.

    d. Enable the **Choose how BitLocker-protected operating system drives can be recovered** policy.

> **Note**: In this procedure, you make sure that the recovery information needed to unlock the drive exists in Active Directory. The recovery password is needed if the password for unlocking BitLocker is lost or the machine has entered BitLocker recovery mode. If you do not save this information, all the data on the drive will be lost if the drive becomes locked.

Activate BitLocker with a Password

1. On **CL02**, log in as **Administrator** in the **VIAMONSTRA** domain.

2. Start an elevated **Windows PowerShell command prompt** (run as administrator) and run the following command:

    > **Enable-BitLocker C: -PasswordProtector –Password $pw –UsedSpaceOnly**

3. When prompted, type the password **Pa$$w0rd** and press **Enter**. Repeat entering the password once more and press **Enter** again.

4. When prompted, restart your computer by typing the following command:

    Restart-Computer

5. While CL02 is restarting, it will prompt you for a password. Enter the password you entered in step 3 to continue the boot.

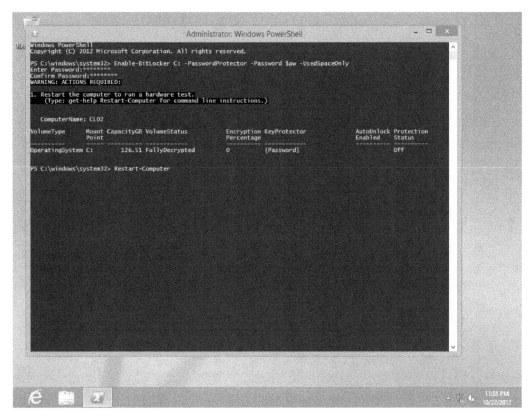

Activate BitLocker on a machine without TPM by using PowerShell.

Note: BitLocker used to be managed by using manage-bde in Windows Vista and Windows 7, but in Windows 8, you also can use PowerShell cmdlets to control BitLocker. You will find more information on PowerShell in Windows 8 in Chapter 7.

Provision BitLocker in WinPE

In all deployments today, you activate BitLocker after the operating system has been installed. One of the really great benefits of Windows 8 is that you can enable BitLocker prior to installing Windows 8, sort of provisioning BitLocker.

When you enable BitLocker on a drive, which takes only seconds, everything will be encrypted on the fly when it is installed. This means little overhead and an encrypted installation the second it is finished.

Note: Provisioning BitLocker in WinPE requires WinPE 4.0, which is a part of ADK

Enterprise Management of BitLocker

I strongly recommend that enterprises using BitLocker also look into Microsoft BitLocker
Administration and Monitoring (MBAM) tool, which is a part of Microsoft Desktop Optimized
Pack. You will find more information about MBAM in Chapter 9.

AppLocker

I must say that AppLocker was my personal favorite security feature when Windows 7 was
launched some years ago, and nothing since then has changed my feelings for AppLocker. It is an
extremely smart way of preventing unwanted stuff from being executed and run on your machines
in an enterprise environment. AppLocker in Windows 8 works the very same way it did in
Windows 7 except that it now offers support for "packaged apps," meaning Windows 8appsthat
come in the Appx format or through Windows Store.

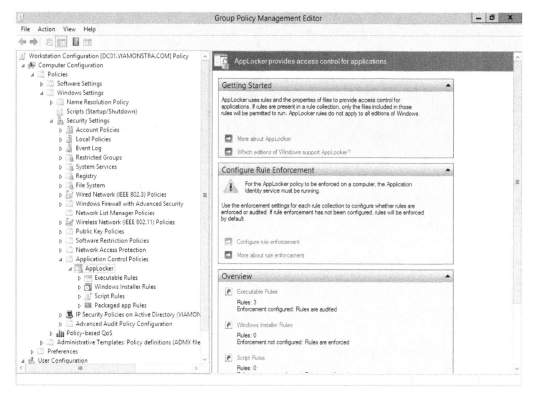

Activating AppLocker is done using a number of Group Policy settings.

Basics of AppLocker

The basics of AppLocker are that you create a whitelist (so-called "allow rules") of what you want to allow to be run on a machine. These can be executable files, Windows Installer files, and scripts of various kinds. Anything that does not meet your allow rules is effectively blocked from executing or running on your client machines, providing very good means for security and minimizing the scenario where users run things they should not.

Starting with Windows 8, you also can control packaged apps, but Windows 8 also introduced control over MST files (transform files for Windows Installer) in addition to rules for MSI and MSP files.

So the following file types can be controlled with AppLocker:

- **Executable**. EXE files

- **Windows Installer**. MSI, MSP, and MST files

- **Scripts**. PS1, CMD, VBS, BAT, and JS

- **DLL**. DLL and OCX

- **Packaged apps**. APPX files or installed packaged apps

> **Real World Note**: More and more applications are being installed in the user profile catalog instead of to Program Files. A few good examples of popular applications that do install without a user having administrative privileges are Google Chrome and Spotify. Using AppLocker will block these types of applications from running (but that of course depends on the rules you create).

The Rules Are Important

AppLocker provides you with three types of rules:

- **Publisher rules**: The most prominent third-party application vendors sign their executable files using a digital certificate, which proves that the executable originates from them and not from any other source. When creating rules, AppLocker will look to see whether there is a digital signature in the application you are trying to allow and then let you use that publisher's information to allow everything from Microsoft Corporation, for instance, to run. Using publisher rules are without a doubt your number one aim when dealing with AppLocker rules, as they require the least amount of administration.

- **Hash rules**: A hash rule means that you make a checksum of a file. The drawback of this is that whenever the file is updated or replaced you need to re-hash and create a new rule that allows that file to be run. From an administrative standpoint, this is not very good as it results in a lot of administration.

- **Path rules**: Last but not least is the path rule. This type lets you create rule to say, for instance, that everything in folder C:\Program files will be allowed to run. This means that if the user can put something in there, it will be allowed to run. Using path rules is your very last option. I strongly recommend against using them, although there are scenarios where using them is all right for specific needs, such as using the default rules.

Strategy

When dealing with AppLocker in enterprises, you need to find a balance between administration and security. Security folks tend to always want the best possible results, meaning a total whitelist where you specify everything. For administrative purposes, this is not always the case because for this to work somewhat well, everything that you want to allow must be signed by a certificate publisher, yourself, or someone you trust.

Signing your in-house applications and converting scripts to PowerShell, and thereby signing those also, will create a secure environment that will improve security and minimize administration when it comes to AppLocker.

Note: One common misconception with AppLocker is that it will control and allow what a user can install, i.e. a standard user is thought to be able to install things if AppLocker allows it. That is false. To be able to install applications (in Program Files), you still need administrative privileges on the machine.

How to Activate AppLocker

Typically three things are required to activate AppLocker: rules, a started service, and setting the enforcement mode. In a real-world scenario, I also recommend that you activate notifications to give your users additional information on why something was blocked from running and the potential means for resolving any issues they encounter.

Configure AppLocker

1. On **DC01**, log in as **Administrator** in the **VIAMONSTRA** domain.

2. Using the **Group Policy Management** console, edit the **Workstation Configuration** group policy.

3. In the **Computer Configuration** / **Policies** / **Windows Settings** / **Security Settings** / **System services** node, double-click the **Application Identity** service.

4. Select the **Define this policy setting** check box, select the **Automatic** option, and then click **OK**.

5. In the same group policy, in the **Computer Configuration** / **Policies** / **Windows Settings** / **Security Settings** / **Application Control Policies** node, double-click **AppLocker**.

6. Right-click **Executable rules** and select **Create default rules**.

Real World Note: The default rules allow everything in Windows to execute. Standard users can potentially copy things to the Windows\Temp folder and execute whatever they need, bypassing AppLocker.

---

7. Double-click **(Default rule) all files located in the Windows folder** and select the **Exceptions** tab.

8. In the **Add exception** drop-down list, choose **Path** and click **Add**.

9. Choose **Browse folders**, browse to **C:\Windows\Temp**, and click **OK** three times.

10. Select the **AppLocker** node and click the **Configure rule enforcement** link.

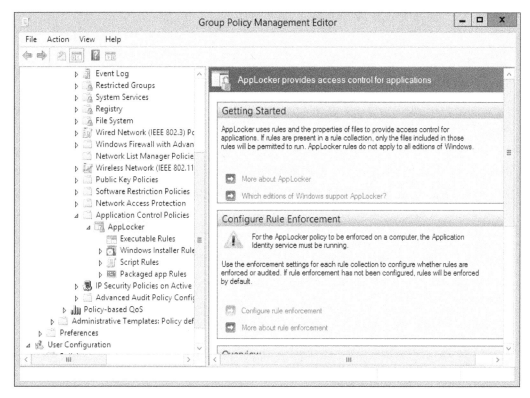

The AppLocker node selected, showing the Configure rule enforcement link.

11. In the **Executable rules** area, select the **Configured** check box, and in the drop-down list, select **Audit only**. Then click **OK**.

Real World Note: The Application Identity service now features the new Windows 8 "trigger start." This means that if the service is stopped for some reason, it will be started automatically the next time something is executed, as long as a set of AppLocker rules has been applied to the machine.

Activate the Web Page with More Support Information

1. On **DC01**, log in as **Administrator** in the **VIAMONSTRA** domain.

2. Using the **Group Policy Management** console, edit the **Workstation Configuration** group policy.

3. In the **Computer Configuration** / **Policies** / **Administrative Templates** / **Windows Components** / **File Explorer** node, enable the **Set a support web page link** policy and configure the following:

> In the **Support Web Page URL** text box, replace the prepopulated URL with **http://dc01/AppLocker.html**, and click **OK**.

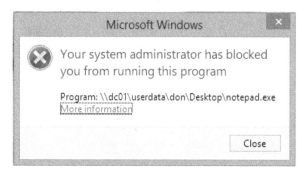

This will be displayed when something is blocked from running; when a support web page URL is entered, there is a "More information" link.

Verify AppLocker Behavior

1. On **CL01**, log in as **Don** in the **VIAMONSTRA** domain.

2. Press the **Windows logo key + R**, type **gpupdate**, and press **Enter**. Wait for the group policy update to finish.

3. Press the **Windows logo key + R** once again and now type **eventvwr.msc** to launch **Event Viewer**.

4. In **Event Viewer**, expand **Applications and Services logs** / **Microsoft** / **Windows** / **AppLocker** / **EXE and DLL**.

5. Investigate the events found there; you should have at least one that says that an **AppLocker policy** has been applied to the system. If not, do another **gpupdate** and wait. Do not close Event Viewer.

6. When AppLocker policies have been applied, start **File Explorer**.

7. Go to **C:\Windows** and open **Notepad.exe**. Verify that the **Event Viewer** (remember to do a refresh to see all new events) shows that Notepad was allowed to run.

8. Copy **Notepad.exe** from **C:\Windows** to the **desktop**.

9. Run **Notepad** from the **desktop** and then look in the **Event Viewer**. You will see a message that states that running Notepad from the desktop would not have been allowed if the AppLocker rules were enforced.

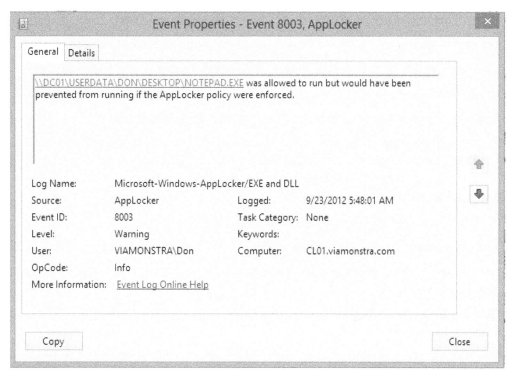

AppLocker in audit mode only logs what would have been prevented from running.

> **Note**: If you are really hardcore, go back to DC01 and change enforcement mode from Audit only to Enforce in the AppLocker settings in Workstation Configuration. Do a gpupdate on CL01 to apply the new set of policies.

Manage AppLocker for Windows 8 Apps

AppLocker rules for Windows 8 apps can be managed in two ways, either by using installed apps or by Appx packages. This requires that you have the book sample files so that you can access the Appx package you used in Chapter 2.

1. On **DC01**, log in as **Administrator** in the **VIAMONSTRA** domain.

2. Mount the **ViaMonstraAppX.iso**.

3. Using the **Group Policy Management** console, edit the **Workstation Configuration** group policy.

4. In the **Computer Configuration / Policies / Windows Settings / Security Settings / Application Control Policies** node, double-click **AppLocker**.

5. Right-click **Packaged app Rules** and choose **Create New Rule**.

6. On the **Before you begin** page, click **Next**.

7. On the **Permissions** page, accept the default settings and click **Next**.

8. On the **Publisher** page, select the **Use a packaged app installer as a reference** option.

9. Click the **Browse** button, browse for the **D:\ViaMonstra.appx** file, and click **Open**.

10. Click **Create**.

11. Select the **AppLocker** node and click **Configure rule enforcement**.

12. In the **Packaged app Rules** area, select the **Configured** check box, and in the drop-down list, select **Enforce rules**. Then click **OK**.

Verify AppLocker for Windows 8 Apps

1. On **CL01**, log in as **Don** in the **VIAMONSTRA** domain.

2. Run **gpupdate** to refresh the group policy.

3. On the **Start screen**, click the **App1** app (the ViaMonstra app). It will start since you have specifically allowed it to run.

4. On the **Start screen**, click the **Mail** app. It will be blocked from running as there is no rule that allows it to run.

5. When you are done, you need to go back and edit the GPO **Workstation Configuration** and set the configuration for **rule enforcement** mode. Otherwise, labs further on in the book will not work as intended. Make sure you set it to **Audit Only** for both **Executable rules** and **Packaged app Rules**.

The message that displays when an app has been blocked from running.

Trusted Boot

In Windows, things have become pretty good from a security standpoint once the machine has booted and you are logged in to the operating system. However, attacks are possible from the time Windows boots up until the necessary protection in the shape, for instance, of anti-malware applications has been loaded into memory and is actively protecting the machine.

With the support for Trusted Boot in Windows 8, that is no longer a problem. Trusted Boot is not a Windows feature per se. Rather, it is a part of UEFI, and Windows 8 supports it. Basically, the firmware (UEFI) stores a list of trusted sources. The boot files are signed by Microsoft, and to be able to boot into Windows 8, the boot files signatures must match what is in the firmware's allow-list.

If they match, the boot proceeds; otherwise, it won't load. It is not very likely that malware will be able to sign their code with a valid signature that exists in the firmware.

Trusted Boot depends on UEFI, and it requires that you to have a machine that supports the newer classes of UEFI. That means you must be able to turn off the compatibility support mode which emulates the old BIOS state in order to use Trusted Boot. Windows 8-certified machines are Trusted Boot compatible.

Early Launch Anti-Malware

Early Launch Anti-Malware (also known as ELAM) is basically an anti-malware driver that is loaded first thing after the Windows kernel has initialized. ELAM is a feature in Windows 8 that makes sure that you have anti-malware protection all the way from the secure boot using Trusted Boot until the machine is ready to log you in.

Verify Trusted Boot State

You can verify the state of Trusted Boot rather easily:

1. On **CL01**, log in as **Administrator** in the **VIAMONSTRA** domain.

2. Press the **Windows logo key + R**, type **msinfo32**, and then press **Enter**.

   Note that in the **Item** column there is an item called **Secure Boot State**, which will tell you the status of Trusted Boot.

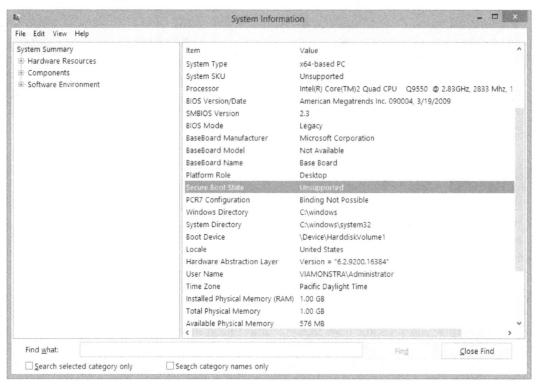

Using msinfo32.exe to find out the Secure Boot State.

Measured Boot Adds Additional Security to Resources

While Trusted Boot adds protection and verification that a machine is clean, there is a second level of security in what is called Measured Boot. It uses TPM to verify that the system client is healthy when, for instance, accessing sensitive data.

Note: Whereas Trusted Boot does not require a TPM chip, Measured Boot does.

Measured Boot requires a third-party validation product. At the time of this writing, there are no announced products for this, although Microsoft is working with multiple vendors. This is not something that Microsoft provides in any of its products.

Virtual Smart Cards

One of the biggest challenges with using smart cards is the cost for the cards themselves and also for supporting and operating the cards and card readers. To the rescue come virtual smart cards that are stored on the hardware, basically in the TPM chips that are found in a full range of corporate computer models for several years now. The support for virtual smart cards is brand new in Windows 8.

Note: The TPM security chip is not activated by default when a machine is delivered from the factory.

Smart cards and virtual smart cards are practically the same in some senses, but in other senses they are not. For instance, a traditional smart card that you hold in your hand is easier to lose or forget. If the card is stolen, it will become locked after a limited number of faulty tries.

Again, virtual smart cards are stored on the machines in the TPM chip and are therefore somewhat easier to attack. Due to the nature of TPM workings, there is only a time delay that limits how many PIN codes you can try; too many faulty tries will only temporarily block the attack.

User Account Control

The infamous User Account Control (UAC) is, of course, also included in Windows 8. I believe that without a doubt UAC was the most unwanted feature introduced with Windows Vista back in the day. Now there isn't that much fuss about UAC, but what many do not know is that UAC actually provides a couple of underlying features that you will miss out on if you turn off UAC.

Extra Value of Using UAC

UAC is so much more than just a dialog box wanting your permission to do things on your machine, it also brings:

- **Application Compatibility**. By default, the activated file and registry virtualization feature comes with UAC. This means that if a standard user runs a legacy application or an application that is not coded well, UAC can redirect writes to a VirtualStore instead of having the application fail in writing, for instance, to the Program Files directory.

- **Internet Explorer extra security**. As long as UAC is active, Internet Explorer will run in so-called protected mode, which is sort of like running in a sandbox, and provide better security.

- **Runas feature**. Whenever a UAC pops up, it allows you to elevate and enter administrator credentials. Because everything is automatic, this is a lot easier to use than "runas" was in Windows XP.

> **Real World Note**: Too often I hear recommendations for turning off UAC, just to make things work. Remember what effects it will have to turn off UAC, and tell any provider, support technician, or developer that turning off UAC is not an option.

UAC in the Enterprise

There is at least one thing to be aware of when dealing with UAC in an enterprise environment. One of the most important things to account for is remote help and support applications, i.e. ensuring that remote control works as expected.

By default, UAC prompts for elevation on something called the secure desktop, and that effectively blocks any remote input. This can be fixed by changing the necessary UAC settings. Note that once again I do not in any way recommend turning off UAC.

Configure UAC to Allow for Remote Support

1. On **DC01**, log in as **Administrator** in the **VIAMONSTRA** domain.

2. Using the **Group Policy Management** console, edit the **Workstation Configuration** group policy.

3. In the **Computer Configuration** / **Policies** / **Administrative Templates** / **Windows settings** / **Security settings** / **Local policies** / **Security Options** node, configure the following:

   a. Disable the **User Account Control: Switch to the secure desktop when prompting for elevation** policy.

   b. Enable the **User Account Control: Allow UIAccess application to prompt for elevation without using the secure desktop** policy.

UAC File and Registry Virtualization in Action

1. On **CL01**, log in as **Don** in the **VIAMONSTRA** domain.

2. Using the **Start screen**, start **Notepad**.

3. Right-click the **taskbar** and select **Task Manager**.

4. Click **More details** if necessary, and on the **Details** tab, right-click **Notepad.exe** and select **UAC virtualization**.

5. In the **Task Manager**, click **Change virtualization**.

6. Switch back to **Notepad**, type anything in the document, and then in the **File** menu, select **Save**.

7. Name the file **UAC.txt**, and save it to **C:\Program files**.

Note: A standard user does not have write permissions to Program Files in a standard-configured Windows 8 machine.

8. Close **Notepad** when done.

9. Using **File Explorer**, navigate to **C:\Program Files**. Note that the **UAC.txt** file is not there.

10. Using **File Explorer**, navigate to **C:\Users\Don\AppData\Local\VirtualStore\Program Files**. You will find the **UAC.txt** file there instead of in C:\Program Files.

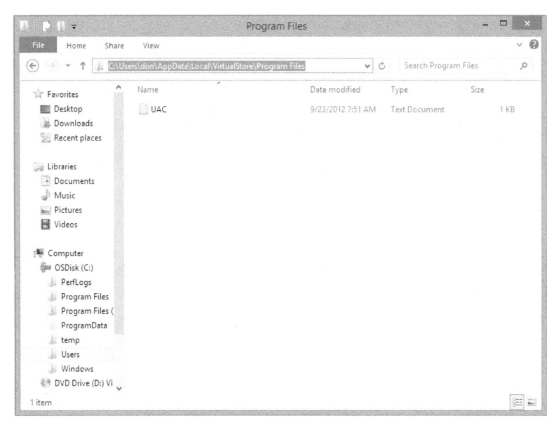

VirtualStore is the location for redirected writes.

Real World Note: Accounts having local administrator privileges normally run as a standard user. But, if you map a network drive and then try to access it, for instance, from an elevated command prompt (using the same user account), you will not see the network mapping. This can be enabled by enabling linked connections. See http://support.microsoft.com/kb/937624 for more information. The KB article refers to Vista and Windows 7 but also applies to Windows 8.

Windows Defender

Windows Defender was something Microsoft acquired from another company about 10 years ago. It was first introduced as an integrated part in an operating system when Windows Vista was released and was available as a separate download for Windows XP. All along, Windows Defender has been a tool that protects you from malware, not from viruses.

A few years ago, Microsoft released Microsoft Security Essentials which does protect you from both malware and viruses. It was the first free tool from Microsoft to do so.

With Windows 8, Microsoft integrates what is known as Microsoft Security Essentials into the operating system. The branding is still Windows Defender, but it now protects you from viruses, as well.

Does this mean that you do not need a third-party anti-virus solution in the enterprise? No. There is still no way to manage Windows Defender centrally or collect reports from the clients, so the need for third-party solutions remains.

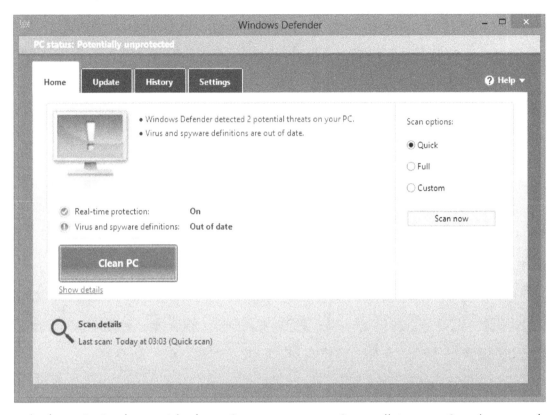

Windows Defender in Windows 8 protects you from all types of malware and viruses·

SmartScreen

SmartScreen is a feature that has existed in Internet Explorer for years. Its purpose historically has been to block users from accessing potentially dangerous web resources containing malware or phishing sites.

Microsoft takes this one step further in Windows 8 and integrates it into the operating system for files that are downloaded from the internet. As a matter of fact, SmartScreen is turned on by default and requires an administrator to approve the file before the user can do anything with it.

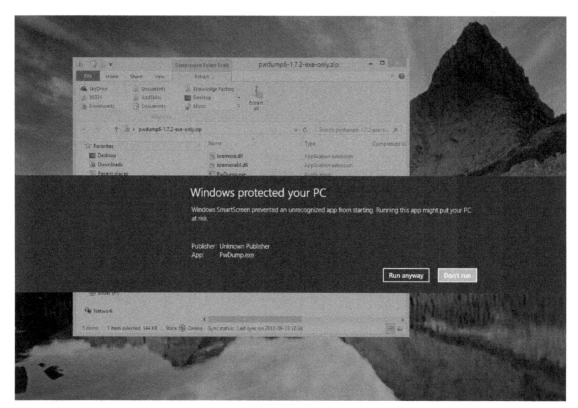

SmartScreen warns that an EXE about to be run might be dangerous.

My opinion on this integration is that it is perfect for the consumer type of users; whereas in the enterprise, you do have a number of other counter-measures for dealing with this kind of threat. You have various perimeter filters, and controlled and (hopefully) updated anti-malware software on the machines. And if you use AppLocker, a SmartScreen filter is of no use to you.

Configure SmartScreen

1. On **DC01**, log in as **Administrator** in the **VIAMONSTRA** domain.

2. Using the **Group Policy Management** console, edit the **Workstation Configuration** group policy.

3. In the **Computer Configuration** / **Policies** / **Administrative Templates** / **Windows Components** / **File Explorer** node, configure the following:

    Enable the **Configure Windows SmartScreen** policy, and configure it to use the **Turn off SmartScreen** setting.

Chapter 5

Virtualization

Virtualization is one area with really interesting new features in Windows 8, and the addition of Client Hyper-V to the already existing Boot from VHD gives many new opportunities. Those two technologies are actually the only technologies in focus in this chapter. Client Hyper-V contains a number of very powerful features.

Client Hyper-V

Hyper-V has been around for a few years now in the Windows Server family of operating systems, making its first appearance in Windows Server 2008. Actually, Hyper-V in Windows 8 is not that different than Hyper-V in Windows Server 2012, as they share the same foundation and features.

For the first time, Microsoft presents a client hypervisor worth the name. This is also the first time that Microsoft has provided the capability to virtualize 64-bit operating systems on a Windows client machine. The fact that Client Hyper-V comes in the box and now contains some substantive features can be a good reason for not using other third-party virtualization products.

Forget Virtual PC or Windows Virtual PC. Client Hyper-V is a real hypervisor in the client OS!

Features

I have an extreme need for running virtual machines when lecturing, presenting workshops, running demos, and so forth. Until Windows 8 came along, I have been forced to use Windows Server 2008 R2 on my laptop, with some drawbacks. All of these drawbacks are actually fixed with Windows 8. Let me take you through some of the excellent features of Client Hyper-V:

- **Snapshots**. The snapshots feature is not new but is very useful for testing things out and jumping back in time. Before testing something that you know might break the system, create a snapshot you can jump back to whenever you have the need for it.

- **Sleep**. In Windows 8, you can put your machine to sleep, and the virtual machines running on it will be saved, as well. This means quick recovery (at least if you are on SSD drives) instead of having to do a complete shutdown and cold boot.

- **Wlan**. Using Client Hyper-V on a laptop means taking full advantage of the wireless network and being able to use WLAN when creating virtual networks in Client Hyper-V. That might seem like a natural thing, but this is new for Windows 8.

- **Touch**. So when you connect to a virtual machine using Hyper-V Manager, it actually uses Remote Desktop Protocol in the background. The Remote Desktop Protocol in Windows 8 has support for touch, so if you have a touch enabled monitor, you also get touch support in your virtual machines (although it will be a little sluggish).

- **Live storage migration**. You can move the storage (VHD or VHDX file) of a running machine to another location on a physical drive or on the network if you are using SMB3. This is really cool and works really well. Moving the storage moves the pieces of data and also replicates any changes until all of them are moved. It then cuts the old storage loose and moves everything to the new location, without any impact on the virtual machine at all—except for performance while doing the move, that is.

- **Virtual disk files on SMB3**. With Client Hyper-V, placing the virtual disk files on an SMB3 share is supported. This means you do not even have to keep the disks local; they can be placed on shared storage somewhere on the network and file servers.

"Developers, Developers, Developers..."

The famous Steve Ballmer quote fits pretty well in the Client Hyper-V chapter because developers are one of the largest groups of users who can benefit most from Client Hyper-V. A developer, sales person, lecturer, and others can have a number of virtualized environments for development or demo purposes. For you in the IT department, Client Hyper-V is a very good tool that you can use to have local test environments for application packaging or just to test changes to the client platform instead of doing it on your production installation.

System Requirements

First off, to be able to use Client Hyper-V, your machine must meet the following criteria:

- Run the 64-bit version of Windows 8 Pro or Enterprise (indirectly demanding 64-bit capable hardware plus hardware-assisted virtualization activated in the BIOS/firmware)

- 4 GB RAM

- SLAT (Second Level Address Translation) support in the CPU

> **Note**: SLAT is not a requirement on Hyper-V in Windows Server 2012, but performance is the reason for SLAT being a requirement on the client, as the usage on a client differs a lot from that on a server operating system.

Check SLAT Support

You have two options for checking whether your machine has support for SLAT. One option is for when you are already running Windows 8 on the machine, and one is for when you are running any other Windows operating system.

Option 1: Already Running Windows 8

To determine the requirements for running Client Hyper-V on a particular model, you perform the following steps on a physical machine rather than a virtual one:

1. On a physical Windows 8 machine, press the **Windows log key** + **R**, type **msinfo32**, and then press **Enter** to start **System Configuration**.

2. Scroll down to the bottom and note that you have a line which tells you the support for **Hyper-V: SLAT**.

3. If the column **Value** reads **Yes**, the machine supports SLAT.

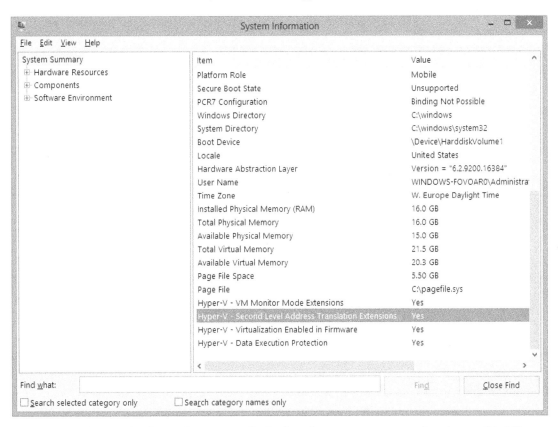

In msinfo32 in Windows 8, you will find information not only about SLAT support but also for other Hyper-V requirements.

Option 2: Running Any Other Windows Operating System Than Windows 8

This option requires the Sysinternals Coreinfo tool that you will find in Tools.iso if you followed the instructions for creating the lab environment in Appendix A.

1. On a physical Windows 8 machine, mount the **Tools.iso** file.

2. Start an elevated **command prompt** (run as administrator).

111

3. Type **cd /d D:\Coreinfo** and press **Enter**.

4. Type **Coreinfo –v** and press **Enter**. This will list your processor's support for SLAT.

   Note what the last line says. An asterisk (*) indicates that the support for SLAT is there.

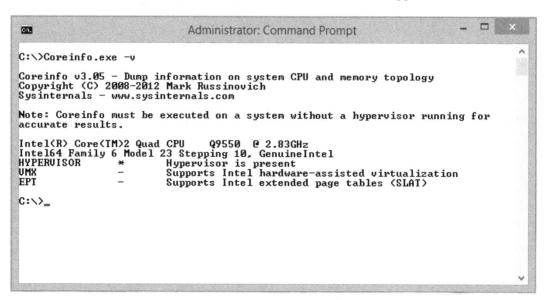

Coreinfo from Sysinternals give you the information you need on SLAT support in the CPU.

Note: Intel and AMD of course have their own naming conventions for basically everything, and this is no exception. If you have an Intel CPU, you should look for Extended Page Tables support (EPT). If you have an AMD CPU, look for Nested Page Tables support (NPT).

How to Deploy Client Hyper-V

Deployment of Client Hyper-V can be done in a number of ways. Using the DISM (Deployment Image Servicing and Management) tool is one of them. You can use this command line to enable Client Hyper-V at OS deployment time (when deploying the machine, for example, using Microsoft Deployment Toolkit) or after deployment.

```
Dism /Online /Enable-Feature /FeatureName:Microsoft-Hyper-V-All
```

This command enables Hyper-V and all of its features, including the management tools with a graphical user interface for creating and managing virtual machines.

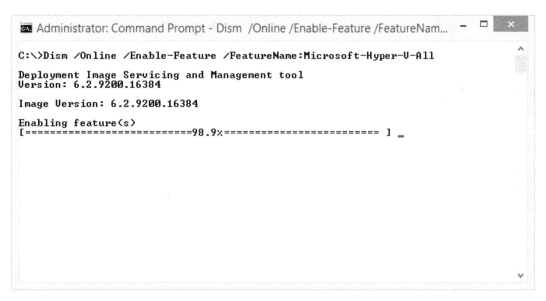

Enabling Hyper-V takes a little time and requires a couple of reboots.

Create a Virtual Machine

This lab requires installing Client Hyper-V on a physical machine that meets the requirements stated earlier in this chapter. To install Hyper-V, use the Dism command mentioned above.

Create a Network

1. On a physical Windows 8 machine, start **Hyper-V Manager** from the **Start screen**.

2. In the **Actions** pane on the right, click **Virtual Switch Manager**.

3. Click **Create Virtual Switch**, and in the **Name** text box, type **Internet**.

4. In the drop-down list under **External networks**, select the network adapter you want to use to share the internet for your virtual machines. Click **OK** when done.

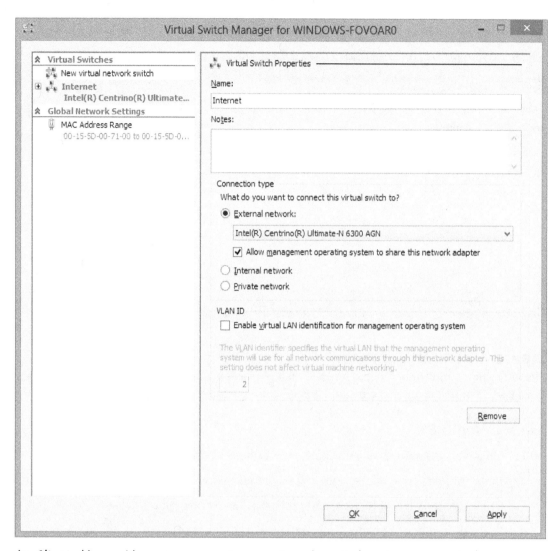

In Client Hyper-V, you can create a network switch using your wireless connection.

Create a Virtual Machine

1. Back in the **Hyper-V Manager** console, in the **Actions** pane, click **New**, and then select **Virtual Machine**.

2. On the **Before You Begin** page, click **Next**.

3. On the **Specify Name and Location** page, enter an appropriate name for your virtual machine, and click **Next**.

> **Note**: If the C drive is full or does not contain several gigabytes (30–40 gigabytes) of free disk space, choose to place the virtual machine on another drive or on a SMB3-enabled file share on the network.

4. On the **Assign Memory** page, give the virtual machine a decent amount of RAM, at least 2 GB static or 1 GB minimum if using Dynamic Memory), and click **Next**. Note that you can use dynamic memory to fit more virtual machines on a host.

5. On the **Configure Networking** page, choose **Internet** in the **Connection** drop-down list, and then click **Next**.

6. On the **Connect Virtual Hard Disk** page, change the location if necessary and click **Next**.

7. On the **Installation Options** page, choose whether you will be booting it from a network or an ISO and then click **Finish**.

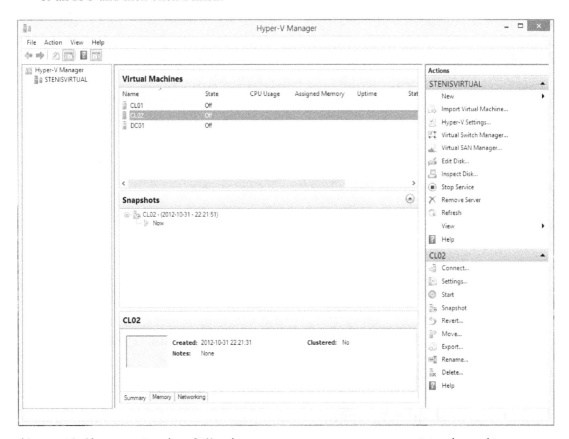

Hyper-V Manager is the GUI where you can manage your virtual machines.

Run a Virtual Machine

In **Hyper-V Manager**, right-click the machine you just started, and choose **Start** to boot the machine and proceed with the installation of the guest operating system. Either use an ISO or do a PXE boot, whichever is applicable in your environment.

Boot from VHD

Another virtualization technique (although it really is not a virtualization technique) is Boot from VHD. With this technique, you create a virtual hard drive file on your local disk and use that virtual hard drive file to boot the machine.

This enables you to have multiple operating systems and switch between them rather easily without having multiple partitions or traditional deployments of Windows. Dual-boot scenarios are not very common or practical in enterprise environments, but Boot from VHD provides an alternative that also can be useful for developers.

In Windows 7, this was a feature for Enterprise customers, but this feature now is also available for Windows 8 Pro users.

> **Note**: So this means that you boot the machine from a single file located on the physical disk. What about performance impact? Well, from my experience, the performance impact is not at all noticeable.

Setting up a Boot from VHD Solution

The steps to set up Boot on VHD are to create a virtual hard drive and mount that. You then put the installation files on the virtual hard drive and indicate in the boot manager that you should be able to boot off this virtual hard driver when starting the machine.

Create the Virtual Hard Drive

1. On **CL01**, log in as **Administrator** in the **VIAMONSTRA** domain.

2. Start an elevated **command prompt** (run as administrator), and type the following commands. Press **Enter** after each command:

   a. **diskpart**

   b. **create vdisk file=C:\W8.vhd maximum=25000 type=expandable**

   c. **select vdisk file=C:\W8.vhd**

   d. **attach vdisk**

   e. **create partition primary**

   f. **assign letter=W**

   g. **format fs=ntfs quick label=W8BootOnVHD**

   h. **exit**

3. Don't close the **command prompt** as it will be used in the next series of steps.

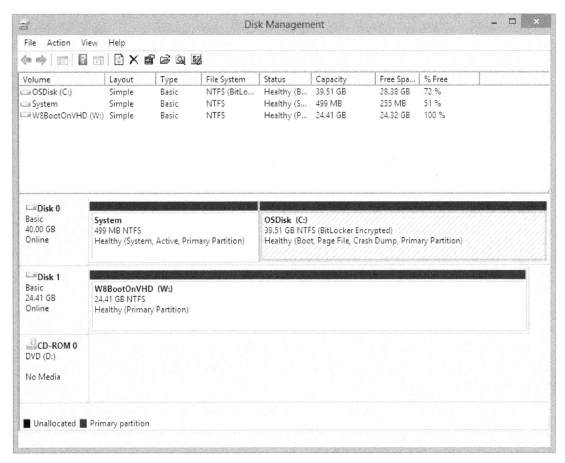

In Disk Management, you also can see the mounted VHD as a separate drive.

Extract Windows Installation Files

These steps require that you have a Windows 8 ISO.

1. On **CL01**, mount the **Windows 8 ISO**.

2. In the previously started **command prompt**, type the following command and press **Enter**:

    Dism /Apply-Image /ImageFile:D:\sources\install.wim /Index:1 /ApplyDir:W:

3. When done applying the image, leave the **command prompt** open.

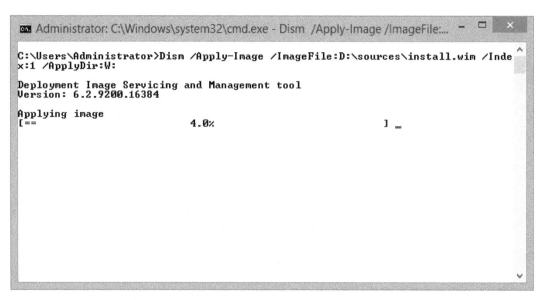

Applying the Windows 8 WIM image using the Dism command.

Make Changes to the Windows Boot Manager

To enable the option of selecting a boot method from the boot menu, you need to write a boot entry using the bcdboot command:

1. In the previously started **command prompt**, type the following command and press **Enter**:

    bcdboot W:\Windows

2. To make this boot entry differ from the normal installation, you need to rename it. First run the following command, and then press **Enter** to look up the correct identifier:

    bcdedit /v

3. Then, to set the new description for the new boot entry, type the following command and press **Enter**. Replace the identifier {guid} with the actual value looked up in step 2:

    bcdedit /set {ab7d37fe-1bc4-11e2-bb92-d83c4ab2bc18} description "Windows 8 Boot on VHD"

4. Leave the **command prompt** open.

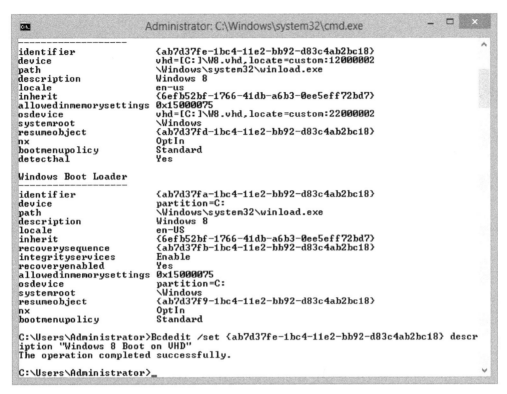

Setting boot entry description using bcdedit.

Boot on the VHD File

1. Restart **CL01** by typing the following command and pressing **Enter**:

   shutdown /r /f /t 0

2. On the **Choose an operating system** menu that appears after rebooting, select **Windows 8 Boot on VHD** to start Windows 8 on the VHD file.

Note: From this point on, it will act like a normal installation of the operating system from the point where the operating system files are already on the disk, which means it will install drivers and configure the OS for the first time.

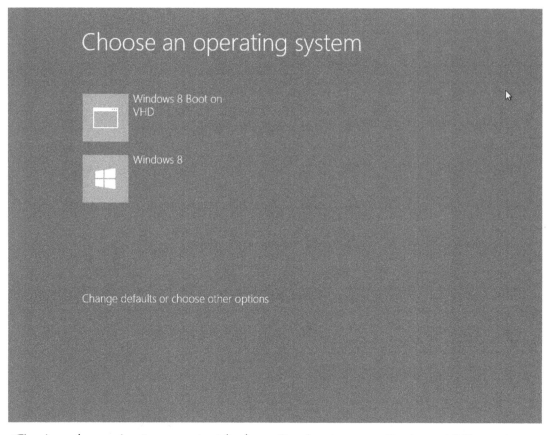

The brand new boot menu in Windows 8, showing our Boot on VHD option.

Chapter 6

Remote Access and Mobility

This chapter is my personal favorite as it contains not only the coolest features but also the most useful ones. A typical user tends to become more and more mobile, and in this chapter, the focus is on new features such as WWAN support and Windows To Go, as well as improved features like DirectAccess and BranchCache.

Windows To Go

Imagine not having to bring your laptop everywhere. Imagine having your personalized installation of Windows 8 on a USB memory stick. That is what Windows To Go delivers. Basically the exact same experience as a traditional Windows installed on a hard drive, only this installation is done on a USB memory stick and thereby also a lot more mobile.

Requirements

To start with, Windows To Go is a feature that comes with Windows 8 Enterprise. When it comes to hardware requirements, Windows To Go is supported only on USB 3.0 devices that are certified for Windows To Go. You cannot simply take any USB memory stick and use it with Windows To Go. That is because you need a drive that reports as a fixed drive in Windows. A typical USB memory stick reports as a removable drive and cannot be partitioned, which is required to use a Windows To Go workspace on machines running in UEFI or BIOS mode.

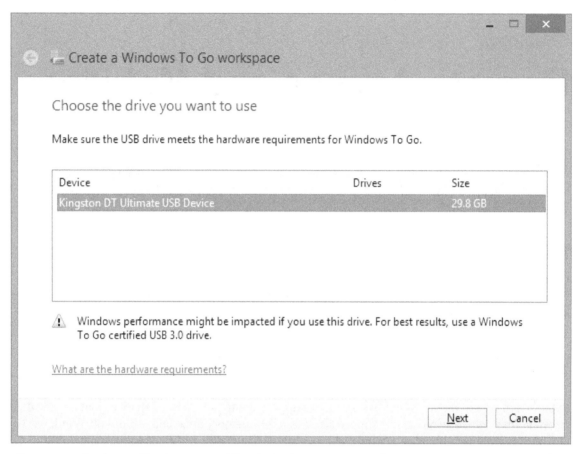

Running Windows To Go on a USB 3·0 device on a USB 2·0 port is supported because all hardware don't support booting using the USB 3·0 port·

Windows To Go is designed to work with KMS or ADBA. Although Windows To Go technically works with MAK activation keys, that is not recommended because MAK keys are tied to the hardware. If a device moves around from one piece of hardware to another, there are obvious problems because your MAK keys will run out pretty fast.

Real World Note: During the Windows 8 beta stage, I (twice) did a three-hour presentation on Windows 8, running on Windows To Go. I ran demos and had three virtual machines running on a four-year old USB 2.0 5400 RPM hard drive. It became a little hot, but it worked like a charm and performance did not suffer noticeably in any way. The point is that Windows To Go works with old drives, but it will work even better with certified drives that are USB 3.0. And remember that only certified devices are supported by Microsoft.

What About Security?

It is no secret that USB memory sticks are very small and tend to have feet, as they are often lost. Running Windows To Go on USB memory sticks is no different, and to account for lost USB memory sticks possibly containing sensitive information, you can use BitLocker with the new password protector to protect the content on the USB memory stick.

Another security feature is that by default you are not able to access the drives of host (physical) machine when using the Windows To Go workspace on that machine. It is recommended to keep it that way, but you can change that by setting a different SAN policy.

How to Create a Windows To Go Workspace

With the Windows To Go tool that is built in to Windows 8 Enterprise, you can create a workspace that enables you to stage your Windows To Go drives to USB devices.

Note: With System Center 2012 Configuration Manager with Service Pack 1, it is possible to let the users provision their own Windows To Go workspaces.

Create a Windows To Go Workspace

1. On a physical Windows 8 Enterprise machine, press the **Windows logo key** + **W**. Start typing **windows to** and then select **Windows To Go** when it displays in the list of search results.

2. Insert a USB device into the physical computer, preferably a USB 3.0 device in a USB 3.0 port, and click **Next**.

Note: Remember that USB memory sticks that are not made specifically for Windows To Go or certified may not work with Windows To Go due to how Windows treat them as removable devices. A USB hard drive of any kind and age will work just fine for this demo, but remember that performance *might* suffer from this and that for production use you should use certified devices.

3. On the **Choose a Windows 8 image** page, click **Add search location** and enter the path to where you have your image (in WIM format) stored. When you have the location, click **Select folder** and it will verify whether it can find a valid image from which to create a Windows To Go device from. When a valid image is found, click **Next**.

Real World Note: Preferably you can use an existing corporate image for Windows To Go, or you might want to pre-stage explicit mobile applications in a separate Windows To Go image.

4. On the **Set a BitLocker password (optional)** page, select the **Use BitLocker with my Windows To Go workspace** check box and enter the password **Pa$$w0rd** twice. Select the **Show my password** check box to verify what you just entered. Click **Next** when done.

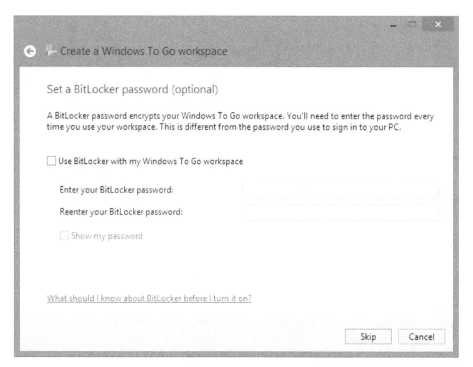

BitLocker can be used together with Windows To Go thanks to the new password protector in BitLocker in Windows 8.

5. On the **Ready to create your Windows To Go workspace** page, click **Create**. Wait until the process is finished; it will take a few minutes.

6. On the **Choose a boot option** page, make sure that **No** is selected, click **Save** and then click **Close**.

Use Your Windows To Go Workspace

Now that you've created your Windows To Go workspace, you need to boot it off a physical machine of your choice.

Insert the USB memory stick in (or connect a USB hard drive to) a physical machine and boot it up.

> **Note**: Make sure that you set the boot order to boot first to USB devices, or set it so that the boot type is selected manually, to ensure that the machine boots to the USB device each time you want to boot to your Windows To Go workspace.

Windows now creates a hardware profile based on unique information on that particular machine and installs the necessary drivers using plug-and-play detection. It is like a normal Windows 8 machine now, and you can do basically everything you can with a traditional installation on a physical hard drive.

> **Note**: Each unique device (machine) will generate a new plug-and-play detection of hardware on its initial boot, causing a boot delay of a couple of minutes on average hardware. That is a once per unique machine thing, though, so the next boot on that same hardware will be immediate.

Challenges with Windows To Go

All new technologies come with challenges, and Windows To Go is no exception. It is beautiful in many ways, but it has its challenges, such as managing drivers and getting users to boot from the USB device.

Driver Management

It's funny that when I talk about deploying Windows, I always recommend separating the drivers for all the computer models you have in your environments. Windows To Go sort of makes you do the opposite. The drivers that are included in Windows 8 cover most of the hardware released up until Windows 8 was RTM. In the long run, however, new hardware models are released and their drivers will be missing. You must be able to handle that, and the way to do it is to put the necessary drivers in the local driver store.

I recommend that you build your own archive of drivers and keep them very structured. My personal preference when storing drivers in the file systems is the following structure:

OS Architecture\Make\Model

An example of this approach is:

Windows 8 x64\Dell Inc.\Precision Workstation M6600.

The local driver store solution, however, only covers running Windows To Go on your corporate machines. Windows To Go also will be run on consumer devices, and the drivers for your corporate machines will not help in that scenario. Keeping a generic driver library of NVIDIA, AMD, and Intel graphics drivers, among others can be a good idea. Also consider letting the Windows To Go workspaces pick up drivers from Windows Update.

Inject Missing Drivers in the DriverStore

To follow this guide, you need either the install.wim from the Windows 8 media or your corporate WIM file. The following steps assume that the WIM file is in C:\Temp and named install.wim, and that your driver library is located in C:\Drivers.

1. On a physical Windows 8 Enterprise machine, download and extract the driver(s) you want to include in your Windows To Go deployment.

> **Note**: To avoid problems with the wrong drivers being offered to the wrong hardware, you should not inject all the drivers into the image that you roll out to other hardware. Also note that the drivers you want to include must be extracted so that you have .inf, .sys, and .cat files. Otherwise the injection will not work.

2. Using **File Explorer**, create a **new folder** in the root of **C:** and name it **Mount**.

3. Start an elevated **command prompt** (run as administrator), and then type the following command and press **Enter** to mount the WIM image:

    Dism /Mount-Wim /WimFile:C:\Temp\install.wim /Index:1 /MountDir:C:\Mount

4. Then type the following command and press **Enter** to inject all drivers in **C:\Drivers** and its subfolders:

    Dism /Image:C:\Mount /Add-Driver /Driver:C:\Drivers /Recurse

5. Finally, type the following command and press **Enter** to unmount the image and save the changes:

    Dism /Unmount-Image /MountDir:C:\Mount /Commit

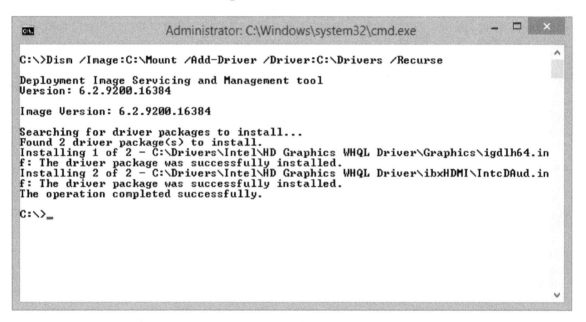

Dism is really good for injecting multiple drivers at once into an image.

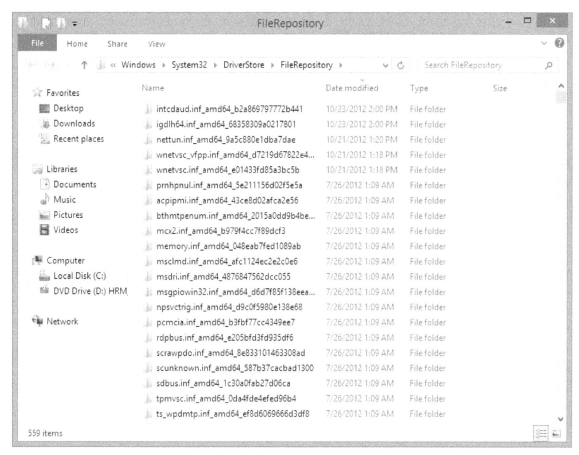

When the drivers have been injected with Dism, they become staged in the DriverStore and can serve plug-and-play detection with drivers when the Windows To Go workspace is started on a machine with that hardware.

USB Boot

For Windows To Go to work, you need to boot from your USB device. On the machines you control in your domain environment, you can set them to boot automatically from Windows To Go if present. But what about the rest of the machines out there, such as those in internet cafés and your users' home environments?

Trying to boot a machine from USB can be a real challenge as you have all kinds of hardware to deal with. On some machines, you press F11, and on others F10, Esc, Del, F1, F2, etc., etc., etc. I'm pretty sure you get the point. Getting your users to achieve this can be easier said than done.

Set USB Boot as the Default

When you are running Windows 8 on your machines and want to be able to use Windows To Go on them, you can activate the group policy to make the computers boot from USB when started.

1. Log in to a domain controller for the domain that your Windows 8 machine is a member of, and start the **Group Policy Management** console.

2. In the OU where the Windows 8 computer account resides, create a new GPO and edit it.

3. In the **Computer Configuration** / **Policies** / **Administrative Templates** / **Windows Components** / **Portable Operating System** node, configure the following:

    Enable the **Windows To Go Default Startup Options** policy.

Note: This Group Policy setting is good for your domain environment. You can instruct your users that if they are running Windows 8, they can search for **Change Windows To Go startup options** and set **Do you want to automatically boot your PC from a Windows To Go workspace** and set it to **Yes**.

USB Memory Sticks Wear Out

Yes, it is true. USB memory sticks wear out rather quickly, so do not expect long lives from your USB devices running Windows To Go. Once again, use certified USB devices to make sure you have the best experience with Windows To Go. You also might want to consider a replacement scheme for your USB memory sticks to avoid potential problems while mobile Windows To Go users are far away from the central office.

Windows Store Disabled by Default

By default, the Windows Store is inactivated on all Windows To Go workspaces. This is because apps are tied to the physical hardware and each app is allowed to be tied to only five physical machines at a time. There is a Group Policy setting you can use to enable this feature if for some reason you do want the Windows Store enabled on your Windows To Go devices. Remember that in enterprises you do not really have a need for this, and any sideloaded app you have will run just fine in Windows To Go as that is not published via the Windows Store.

WWAN and Metered Connections

Mobile connections have become very popular over the last few years, but a big challenge remains around cost as you often have a limited quota for data transfer or have to pay based on how much data is transferred. You therefore want to manage the use of costly connections as much as possible to lower or at least control the costs. Windows 8 introduces what is called metered connections for WWAN types such as 3G and 4G (and also for Wi-Fi connections if you should have the need for that).

You can activate metering on any mobile connection, and that means, for instance, that updates from Windows Update will not be downloaded by default (if they are not critical) and some Windows 8 apps might deliver another "lighter" experience when running on a metered connection.

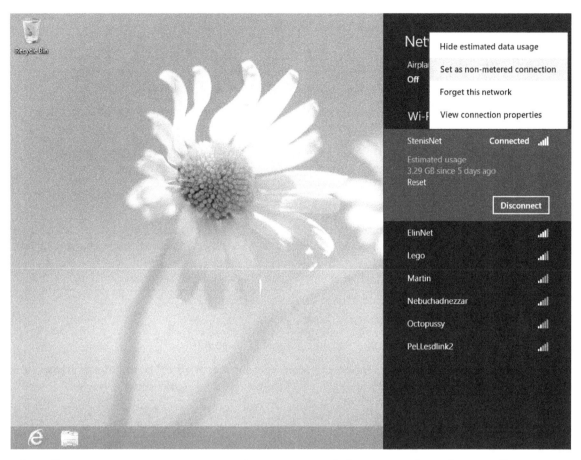

For all connections, you can see the amount of data transferred, as well as set a connection as metered.

> **Real World Note**: Another thing to notice, and something that will make you in the IT department happy, is that Microsoft has developed in cooperation with the Swedish communication company Ericsson a protocol that enables WWAN devices to work without additional third-party drivers. The WWAN devices will just work, provided that the devices meet the requirements and are not too old. From a deployment perspective, WWAN devices are among the most troublesome to deploy for Windows 7 and earlier versions of Windows.

Different Types of Usage Plans

Mobile connections have various cost models. Accordingly, you can set your connections to one of usage plan modes:

- **Unrestricted**. For connections with unlimited access or no restraints.
- **Fixed**. For connections that are not charged or costed per byte up to a certain amount; for instance, some accounts allow up to 1 GB per month. This is the default option for WWAN connections in Windows 8.

- **Variable**. For connections that cost per byte.

Configure the Cost

1. On **DC01**, log in as **Administrator** in the **VIAMONSTRA** domain.

2. Using the **Group Policy Management** console, edit the **Workstation Configuration** group policy.

3. In the **Computer Configuration** / **Policies** / **Administrative Templates** / **Network** / **WWAN Service** / **WWAN Media Cost** node, configure the following:

   Enable the **Set 3G Cost** policy, and then select the **Variable** option.

Note: There are corresponding Group Policy settings for Set 4G Cost and Set Cost for WLAN. There also is a setting, "Set default download behavior," for BITS jobs on costed networks that lets you define how BITS behaves on costed networks; another setting is "Enable file synchronization on costed networks," as mentioned in Chapter 3.

Verify the Data Transfer Amount

1. Press **Ctrl** + **Shift** + **Escape** to bring up **Task Manager**.

2. Click the **App History** tab, and sort by clicking the **Network (MB)** column or **Metered network (MB)** column to see exactly which apps are costing the most.

DirectAccess

DirectAccess is one of the most effective remote connection solutions, and it comes for free in Windows Server 2012 and Windows 8 Enterprise. It was introduced in Windows 7 and Windows Server 2008 R2 and was improved in the following Service Pack 1, as well as through the connectivity assistant that is available to assist when troubleshooting remote connections.

The main purpose of DirectAccess is to provide transparent remote connection to the users. With DirectAccess, they only need to have an active internet connection to be able to access internal resources. The IT department, on the other hand, can deploy group policies, apply software packages, provide updates, perform remote management, and more on the clients regardless of where they are in the world.

However, there have been a lot of challenges around DirectAccess. For instance, DirectAccess in Windows Server 2008 R2 must have two consecutive external IP addresses, and other challenges include the need for an IPv6 resource on the inside to be able to access applications and, last but not least, load balancing. To really use DirectAccess in an enterprise environment, you need to have additional servers running Forefront UAG (Unified Access Gateway) to get IPv6 to IPv4 translation and load balancing.

DirectAccess in Windows Server 2012 Removes Obstacles

In Windows Server 2012, Microsoft has taken a new grip on remote access and thrown in a new role called Remote Access. This new role configures both VPN and DirectAccess. Also, a truly amazing fact is that all the features from UAG are put into the core operating system in Windows Server 2012. What this means in practice is that if you get a license for Windows Server 2012, you can run fully featured DirectAccess in a setup that requires no additional licenses or costs.

DirectAccess also adds support for the use of virtual smart cards for authentication, which is very useful.

Two Modes to Set Up on the Server Side

In addition to the need for two consecutive IP addresses (which is no longer required in DirectAccess, at all), some smaller businesses have faced another challenge. Many have found it complicated to set up DirectAccess. Therefore, Microsoft added an additional quick setup mode to make it easier for customers that don't have the resources for the standard setup, which means you now have two to choose from:

- **Quick mode**. The quick mode is the default and what I would call "quick and dirty." It will get you up and running, but the best option if possible is to configure DirectAccess fully. Quick mode is really intended for small businesses and not enterprises.

- **Full mode**. The full mode is the original and best option in terms of security and control. It requires more in the form of a PKI infrastructure and has a few more manual steps, but is a longer term enterprise solution.

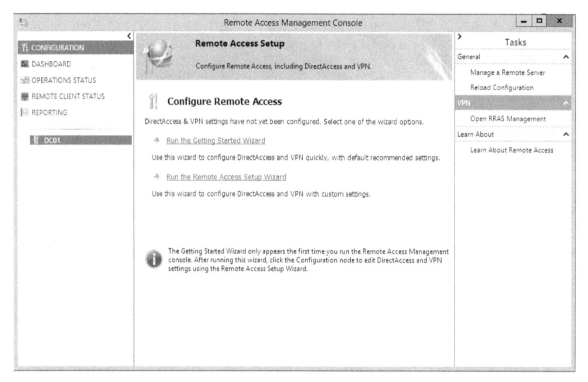

Two setup modes are available for setting up DirectAccess; both are available in the Remote Access Management console.

How to Set Up DirectAccess in Quick Mode

Setting up DirectAccess in quick mode requires very little effort, and the steps are to run the DirectAccess guide, activate it, and then make sure that the Windows 8 clients get the necessary configuration through group policies.

Set Up Direct Access on the Server

1. On **DC01**, log in as **Administrator** in the **VIAMONSTRA** domain.
2. Using **Server Manager**, click **Add roles and features**.
3. If the **Before you begin** page is displayed, select the **Skip this page by default** check box and click **Next**.
4. On the **Select installation type** page, select **Role-based or feature-based installation**.
5. On the **Select destination server** page, select **DC01.viamonstra.com** and click **Next**.
6. On the **Select server roles** page, select the **Remote Access** role.
7. In the **Add Roles and Features Wizard** dialog box, select **Add Features**, and then click **Next**.

132

8. On the **Select features** page, accept the default settings and click **Next**.

9. On the **Remote Access** page, click **Next**.

10. On the **Select role services** page, accept the default settings and click **Next**.

11. On the **Web Server Role (IIS)** page, click **Next**.

12. On the **Select role services** page, accept the default settings and click **Next**.

13. On the **Confirm installation selections** page, click **Install**.

14. When the installation is completed, on the **Installation progress** page, click the **Open the Getting Started Wizard** link.

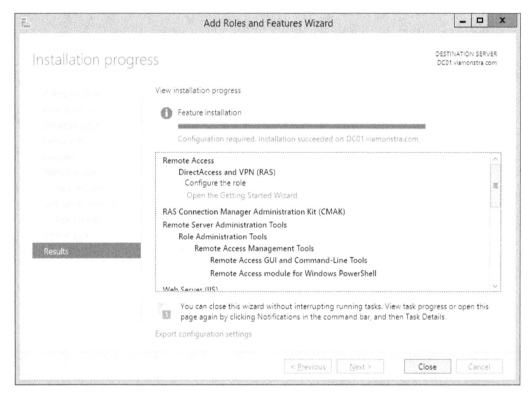

The Installation progress page showing the Open the Getting Started Wizard link.

15. On the **Configure Remote Access** page, click **Deploy DirectAccess only**. Wait for the prerequisites check to finish; it will not take long.

16. On the **Remote Access Server Setup** page, configure the following:

    a. Make sure that the default **Behind an edge device (with a single network adapter)** option is selected.

        b. In the **Type the public name or IPv4 address used by clients to connect to the Remote Access server** text box, type **directaccess.viamonstra.com**.

        c. Click **Next**.

17. Now everything is set for a DirectAccess deployment, but you do want to verify what will happen when you click Finish. On the **Configure Remote Access** page, click the link **here** to view the configuration of DirectAccess that will be applied.

18. Explore the configuration and note that you have the opportunity to change most settings. When you are finished exploring the configuration page and settings, click **OK**.

19. On the **Configure Remote Access** page, click **Finish**.

20. When the **Applying Getting Started Wizard Settings** message is displayed, select **More details** to see what is happening in detail. Watch what happens and wait for everything to finish.

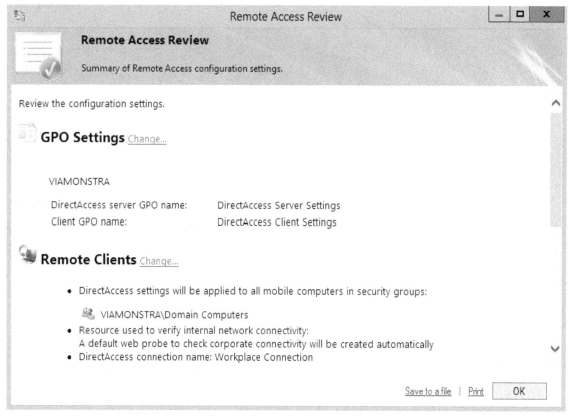

Even in quick setup mode you have the possibility to change many of the settings before finishing and applying the DirectAccess configuration.

> **Note**: Due to the nature of our limited lab environment, I will not take the DirectAccess setup further than this. The purpose of this demonstration was to show how easy it is to get going with DirectAccess in the new quick mode. I recommend this setup for anyone doing a proof-of-concept solution for your company or another company if you are in the consulting business. If you want to configure Direct Access in full mode, you choose the link Run the Remote Access Setup Wizard and then choose Deploy Direct Access Only.

BranchCache

If you have branch offices, and in particular if they have slow WAN connections to headquarters or the hosting partner, then BranchCache can be really useful to you. What it does is allow users in the branch office to cache content that is hosted at headquarters or the hosting partner, making subsequent access to the content significantly faster for the branch users.

BranchCache was introduced in Windows 7 and Windows Server 2008 R2 but has been improved in Windows 8 and Windows Server 2012 to further enhance performance and caching.

> **Note**: Although you can use BranchCache in Windows 8 with content servers running Windows Server 2008 R2, I strongly recommend that to get the absolutely best performance and user experience that you use Windows Server 2012 to host the content that will be cached in your branch office.

BranchCache Features

BranchCache can cache content using the most common protocols out there. This includes SMB, HTTP(S), and BITS traffic. That means you can cache all content from your file servers, content from your web servers, and also your servers using BITS.

This includes caching for System Center Configuration Manager (ConfigMgr) distributing points, Offline Address Book in Exchange, and Windows Server Update Services (WSUS) updates. In particular, BranchCache with WSUS is really good solution that ensures that you do not have your branch office clients fetching a large number of security and other updates via your centralized WSUS server. Having the WSUS content cached in the branch office also gets the updates to all clients more quickly.

BranchCache Comes in Two Flavors

BranchCache is available in two setup modes. The one you use depends on the number of clients at the branch office, as well as the mobility of the users at the branch office.

Distributed Cache Mode

Distributed cache mode is a solution that enables caching on any client in the branch office. When you configure BranchCache using this mode, the clients in the branch office can cache content that is available to other clients, or retrieve something already cached by another client in the branch. This works well for branches with a small number of clients and whose users aren't highly mobile.

Hosted Cache Mode

If you have a larger number of users at a branch office, or if the users are very mobile, you will likely benefit from dedicating a server to act as a cache server. That means everything is retrieved from the main office or hosting partner and cached at a server from which the clients in that branch office then fetch the data.

> **Real World Note:** Activating BranchCache in distributed cache mode is "free" in the sense that you already have everything in place in the branch office. Try that first and then evaluate whether you need to use a dedicated server in hosted cache mode in the branch office.

With Windows 8 and Windows Server 2012, you have the option to combine the settings for branch offices with hosted cache and branches with distributed cache . This is made possible by registering a Windows Server 2012 BranchCache server as a Service Connection Point (SCP) to Active Directory.

Backward Compatibility

The changes made to BranchCache in Windows Server 2012 and Windows 8 result in significant differences when compared to Windows 7 and Windows Server 2008 R2. The optimizations done to the file-hashing mechanism are so great that the new BranchCache is not compatible with the older version. However, BranchCache in Windows Server 2012 by default generates hashes in both v1 format (for Windows 7 and Windows Sever 2008 R2) and in v2 format (for Windows 8 and Windows Server 2012). You also can force the use of v2 hashing only via group policies.

How to Activate BranchCache

Prepare the File or Content Server for BranchCache

1. On **DC01**, log in as **Administrator** in the **VIAMONSTRA** domain.

2. Using **Server Manager**, select **Add roles and features**.

3. If the **Before you begin** page is displayed, select the **Skip this page by default** check box and click **Next**.

4. On the **Select installation type** page, select **Role-based or feature-based installation**.

5. On the **Select destination server** page, select **DC01.viamonstra.com** and click **Next**.

6. On the **Select server roles** page, expand the **File and Storage Services (Installed)** node, expand the **File and iSCSI Services (Installed)** node, select **BranchCache for network files**, and click **Next**.

7. On the **Select Features** page, select **BranchCache** and click **Next**.

8. On the **Confirm installation selections** page, click **Install**.

Chapter 6   Remote Access and Mobility

> **Note**: There are two BranchCache options that you can add. The first is found under Roles and is for servers that host shared folders—for example, a file server (SMB protocol). The second option is found under Features and is intended for content servers, such as web or ConfigMgr distribution points (HTTP(S) and BITS protocol traffic), or when you deploy a server that acts as a hosted cache mode server.

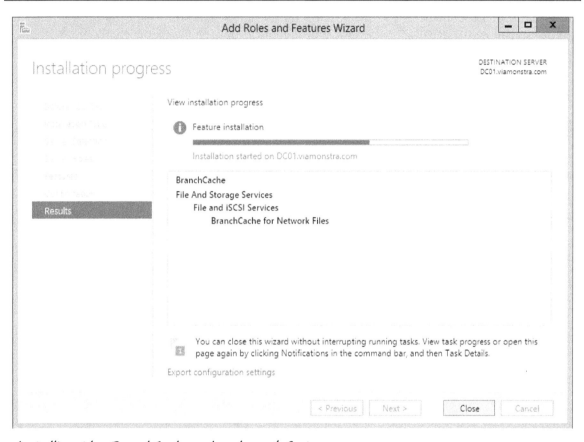

Installing the BranchCache sub-role and feature.

Set Necessary Settings to Activate BranchCache on a Shared Folder

1. On **DC01**, log in as **Administrator** in the **VIAMONSTRA** domain.

2. Using the **Group Policy Management** console, edit the **Default Domain Policy** group policy.

3. In the **Computer Configuration** / **Policies** / **Administrative Templates** / **Network** / **Lanman Server** node, configure the following:

   Enable the **Hash Publication for BranchCache** policy. Configure the policy settings and select **Allow hash publication only for shared folders on which BranchCache is enabled**.

> **Note**: Setting the group policy for hashing is only applicable to file servers. It is not a requirement to activate BranchCache for web servers (also referred to as content servers).

Activate BranchCache for a Share

This lab requires that you mount the ISO file Tools.iso to DC01. The virtual DVD drive is expected to be D:. In these steps, you add content to a shared folder for which you enable BranchCache. You manually run the hashgen command to generate hashes instantly for the files so they are available immediately for caching on your distributed clients later on in the lab.

1. On **DC01**, log in as **Administrator** in the **VIAMONSTRA** domain.

2. Mount the **Tools.iso** file.

3. Using **File Explorer**, create a folder named **BranchCacheShare** in the root of the **C:** drive.

4. Right-click the **BranchCacheShare** folder and choose **Properties**.

5. Go to the **Sharing** tab and click **Advanced Sharing**.

6. Select the **Share this folder** check box and click the **Caching** button.

7. Select the **Enable BranchCache** check box, click **OK** twice, and then click **Close**.

8. Using **File Explorer**, navigate to the **D:\ADK\Installers** folder and copy the **WPTx64-x86_en-us.msi** file to **C:\BranchCacheShare**.

> **Note:** The WPTx64-x86_en-us.msi file is only a sample file to demonstrate the BranchCache functionality. You could use any file.

9. Start an elevated **command prompt** (run as administrator), type the following command, and press **Enter**:

    hashgen C:\BranchCacheShare

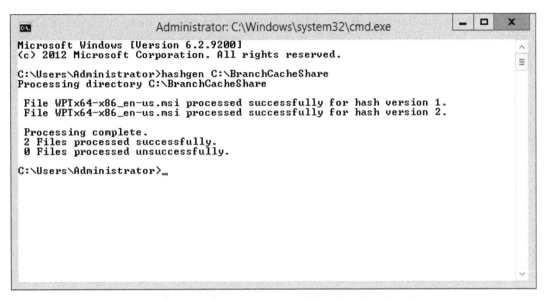

The hashgen command-line utility generated both v1 and v2 hashes.

Configure the Windows 8 Client

All that needs to be configured on the client are a few Group Policy settings.

1. On **DC01**, log in as **Administrator** in the **VIAMONSTRA** domain.

2. Using the **Group Policy Management** console, edit the **Workstation Configuration** group policy.

3. In the **Computer Configuration** / **Policies** / **Administrative Templates** / **Network** / **BranchCache** node, configure the following:

   a. Enable the **Configure BranchCache for network files** policy. Configure the **Type the maximum round trip network latency (milliseconds) after which caching begins** setting to **0**.

Note: For demonstration purposes, latency is set to 0 in this lab; otherwise, the demonstration will not work unless you are using a WAN emulator. In a real environment, the default 80 milliseconds work well in most cases.

---

   b. Enable the **Set BranchCache Distributed Cache mode** policy.

   c. Enable the **Turn on BranchCache** policy.

4. In the **Computer Configuration** / **Policies** / **Administrative Templates** / **Windows Settings** / **Security Settings** / **Windows Firewall with Advanced Security** / **Windows Firewall with Advanced Security** / **Inbound rules** node, configure the following:

   a. Right-click **Inbound rules** and choose **New Rule**.

139

    b.   Click **Predefined** and in the drop-down list, choose **BranchCache – Peer Discovery (Uses WSD)**; then click **Next**, **Next**, and **Finish**.

    c.   Right-click **Inbound rules** again and choose **New Rule**.

    d.   Click **Predefined** and in the drop-down list, choose **BranchCache – Content Retrieval (uses HTTP)**; then click **Next**, **Next**, and **Finish**.

Verify That It Works

1. On **CL01**, log in as **Administrator** in the **VIAMONSTRA** domain.

2. Run a **gpupdate** to refresh the policy you changes you made in the preceding configuration steps.

3. Start **Performance Monitor** by pressing the **Windows logo key + R**, type in **perfmon**, and press **Enter**.

4. In the **Performance Monitor** tool, select the **Performance Monitor** node (which is the sub-node to Monitoring Tools).

5. Click the arrow on the **Change graph type** button (the third button from the left), or press **Ctrl + G**, and then choose **Report**.

6. Click the **green plus sign** just to the right of the **Change graph type** button.

7. In the **Available counters** list, select **BranchCache**, and then click **Add** followed by **OK**.

8. Start **File Explorer** and navigate to the \\dc01\BranchCacheShare folder.

9. Copy the file **WPTx64-x86_en-us.msi** to the root of **C:**.

Note: Look in Performance Monitor and watch SMB: Bytes served from the server. It is expected behavior for all data to be fetched from the server, as this is the first client accessing the data.

---

10. On **CL02**, log in as **Administrator** in the **VIAMONSTRA** domain.

11. Repeat steps 2–9 on **CL02**.

Note that in Performance Monitor on CL02, SMB: Bytes from cache has a value that corresponds to the data amount that was transferred.

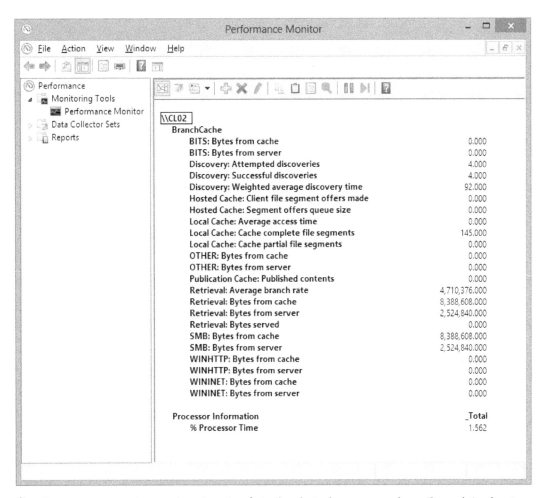

Performance counters showing in detail what happens when BranchCache is active.

Chapter 7

Management

When you have all the client pieces in place, it is time for the management and operations parts. Although Windows 8 is working really well and is stable, you can expect that sooner or later you will run into problems. It is absolutely necessary to manage your clients in an enterprise environment. This chapter focuses on management tools and how to deal with group policies, ActiveX installations, and, last but definitely not least, PowerShell.

Remote Server Administration Tools

Regardless of whether you are managing Windows clients or Windows servers, there are many tools you just cannot miss out on. They are a part of Remote Server Administration Tools (RSAT) and include management consoles for all server features. The consoles include, for instance, the Group Policy Management console, Active Directory Users and Computers snap-in, DNS Management console, and many more.

The trick is that you install RSAT on your Windows 8 client and use the tools from there to manage group policies, users, security groups, DNS, DHCP, and so forth. This is much more efficient than logging into each server through Remote Desktop and then managing whatever you are trying to manage from that particular server.

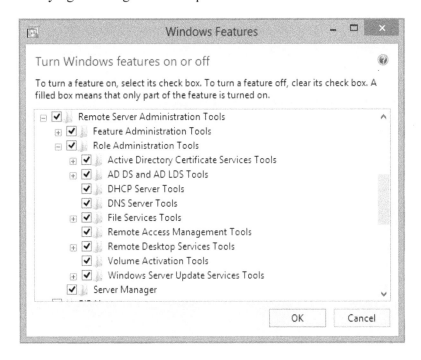

Included with RSAT are a great number of tools that allow you to manage all server features.

All Management Consoles Are Installed with RSAT

When you installed RSAT for Windows Vista or Windows 7, the tools were not actually installed during that installation. You had to enable them manually before you could use any of the management consoles. In RSAT for Windows 8, it is the complete opposite—all management consoles are enabled by default.

Install Remote Server Administration Tools

This lab assumes that you have created the Tools.iso as part of the Appendix A instructions.

1. On **CL01**, log in as **Administrator** in the **VIAMONSTRA** domain.

2. Mount the **Tools.iso** file.

3. Using **File Explorer**, navigate to the **D:\RSAT for Windows 8** folder and install **RSAT** by starting the **Windows6.2-KB2693643-x64.msu** update. Use the default settings for the installation.

4. When **RSAT** is installed, press the **Windows logo key** to go to the **Start screen**.

5. On the **Start screen**, press the **Windows logo key + C** to bring up the **charms**, and then click **Settings**.

> **Real World Note:** Because you opened the charms while the Start screen was displayed, the settings displayed the Tiles option directly. If you had opened the charms directly from the desktop, the settings would have displayed differently.

6. Click **Tiles**, and under **Show administrative tools**, set the flip switch to **Yes**.

7. Go back to the **Start screen** and watch it fill with management consoles.

When showing administrative tools on the Start screen, it fills up quickly.

Group Policies

Windows 8 introduces many new Group Policy settings and, with those, a number of new ADMX and ADML files. There are some Group Policy topics that are particularly useful for purposes of working with Windows 8 in enterprise environments. This section provides a glimpse into how to work with group policies in such environments..

Central Store

Having a central store for group policies will make the lives of everyone who manages group policies in your organization easier. Why? Because if you create a central store, you put all your Group Policy template files (ADMX and ADML) in one location and make sure that everyone is using the same files.

Take, for instance managing, Office Group Policy settings where the policy definitions (ADMX files) are not available by default. You need to download them and add them to the Group Policy Management console when you want to edit an Office setting. If you do that on your machine and then a colleague of yours wants to edit that GPO from another machine, your colleague will see your Office settings as "Extra registry settings" as they lack the Office policy definitions in their local store.

Instead, copying those policy definition files to the central store ensures that everyone managing group policies will use the same policy definitions.

> **Note**: By default, the Group Policy Management console is designed to look for a central store of policy definitions in the SYSVOL share (for example, \\viamonstra.com\SYSVOL\ viamonstra.com\Policies\PolicyDefinitions). If a central store of group policies is not found, the console uses the content of the local PolicyDefinitions folder.

Create (or Update) the Central Store

1. On **CL01**, log in as **Administrator** in the **VIAMONSTRA** domain.

2. Using **File Explorer**, navigate to **C:\Windows**, and copy the entire **PolicyDefinitions** folder to **\\viamonstra.com\sysvol\viamonstra.com\Policies**.

> **Real World Note**: The preceding steps are also valid if you already have a central store in place for previous operating system versions. In such cases, you need to replace the contents in PolicyDefinitions in the SYSVOL share with all ADMX and ADML files from a Windows 8 machine.

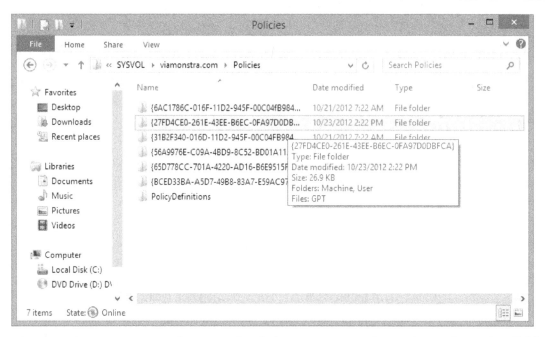

A central store is actually just the PolicyDefinitions being housed in the SYSVOL share.

Verify the Central Store Operation

1. On **CL01**, log in as **Administrator** in the **VIAMONSTRA** domain.

2. Using the **Group Policy Management** console, edit the **Workstation Configuration** group policy.

3. In the **Computer Configuration / Policies** node, select **Administrative Templates**.

4. Note what the title says. When central store templates are being used, it says **Administrative Templates: Policy definitions (ADMX files) retrieved from central store**. Close the **Group Policy Management Editor**.

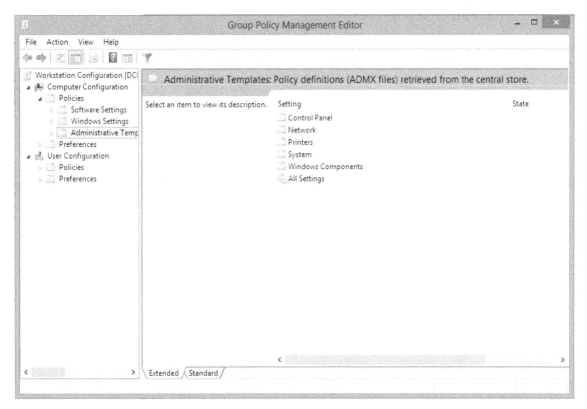

In the Group Policy Management Editor, you will see under Administrative Templates whether the policy definitions were loaded from the local store or the central store·

Finding the Group Policy Settings Easily

With every new version of Windows, a number of new Group Policy settings are introduced. Windows 8 is no different, and now there are literally thousands of settings that you can set using group policies. The more settings, the harder to find what you need by just looking around in the Group Policy editor. New filtering possibilities in the Group Policy Editor come to the rescue.

Filter and Find Relevant Group Policy Settings

1. On **CL01**, log in as **Administrator** in the **VIAMONSTRA** domain.

2. Using the **Group Policy Management** console, edit the **Workstation Configuration** group policy.

3. Expand the **Computer Configuration** / **Policies** / **Administrative Templates** node, and select **All Settings**.

4. Right-click **All Settings** and select **Filter Options**.

5. Select the **Enable Keyword Filters** check box; in the **Filter for word(s)** input area, type **BitLocker** and then click **OK**.

   Now all Group Policy settings which matched BitLocker are listed. You can see whether they are set and where the settings are found in the settings tree path.

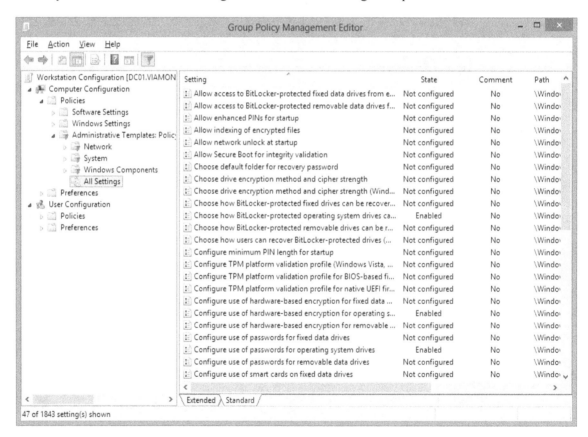

Filtering is a really good way to quickly find GPO settings.

Note: There is also the Group Policy reference sheet in Excel format that you can use to see all settings, which operating systems they apply to, and also which settings are new to Windows 8 and Windows Server 2012. Not all new Group Policy settings are only for the newer OSs; they can work for earlier Windows versions, as well.

The Challenge of User Settings

How to deal with user Group Policy settings is a rather common question and one that I would say all companies have experienced when migrating to another Windows version. The scenario is the following: how do you handle user Group Policy settings when you have multiple operating systems, such as Windows XP and Windows 7, and you are introducing a second or third operating system such as Windows 8?

First, I strongly recommend that you do not reuse the configuration you have for Windows XP for Windows 7 or Windows 8. Group policies tend to grow over time, and I have found that most customers have a lot of rubbish in their old configurations. Starting over and migrating only what is needed minimizes the risk for problems and makes the configuration slicker and easier to manage in the long run.

There are a few options to ensure that users get the right configuration when they log in to Windows XP, for instance, and another configuration when they log in to a Windows 7 or Windows 8 machine. Let's have a look at these options, including the pros and cons and followed by recommendations from the field.

Real World Note: Although you also could use security group filtering or move the users to another OU, these options require a lot of administration and are often bound to break other dependencies because the user accounts are expected to be in a particular OU, for example.

WMI Filters

Windows Management Instrumentation (WMI) filters can be set on any Group Policy objects to control what they are applied for. When you separate user configuration between different Windows versions, you check the OS version to determine which set of group policies are applied to what operating system.

Pros of Using WMI Filtering on Group Policy Objects

- You can keep the user accounts in the OU where they are today, not affecting other services or applications that rely on users being in a certain OU.

- It is a long-term investment in making it easy to introduce new operating system versions and keeping the configurations separated.

- It provides a quick determination of whether the GPO should be applied. (WMI is often accused of being very slow, but the query you use to see check the OS version is not performance intensive.)

Cons of Using WMI Filtering on Group Policy Objects

- You need to implement changes for your existing environment. For instance, Windows XP or Windows 7 user configurations need to have WMI filters applied to make sure those policies do not get into the Windows 8 platform.

- It can prevent group policies from being applied due to problems with the WMI repository or related services.

Loopback Processing

Loopback processing means that you create a number of user Group Policy settings and place them in the OU for Windows 8, for example. You then apply loopback processing which means that when a particular user logs in to a Windows 8 machine, it will also process the user group policies that you have in that OU.

Pros of Using Loopback Processing on Group Policy Objects

- You can keep the user accounts in the OU where they are today, not affecting other services or applications that rely on users being in a certain OU.

- It is a very reliable solution.

Cons of Using Loopback Processing on Group Policy Objects

- If Replace mode is not used, you need to handle the current user configurations in some way.

- It might become difficult to troubleshoot and maintain if naming and configuration are not done consistently and clearly.

> **Real World Note**: Sometimes I recommend WMI filters for separating user settings depending on what operating system they are logging in to, and sometimes I recommend loopback processing. It depends on the environment and needs of the customer. Many times, moving user accounts around in the OU structure is not an alternative, but I consider that to be a very good alternative whenever you can do it.

Implement WMI Filtering for Group Policies

In the Group Policy Management console, you create a WMI filter for each operating system for which you want to separate the user settings. You then set each WMI filter on the GPOs that contain user settings for each operating system, respectively.

> **Note**: Always test this configuration before applying it to your existing production environment. Also note that this does not affect performance noticeably.

The following WMI queries ask the WMI class Win32_OperatingSystem to check and match for the version number of the operating system and also the product type, for which 1 means it is a Windows client machine:

WMI query for Windows XP:

```
SELECT * FROM Win32_OperatingSystem WHERE Version LIKE "5.2%" AND
ProductType ="1"
```

WMI query for Windows 7:

```
SELECT * FROM Win32_OperatingSystem WHERE Version LIKE "6.1%" AND
ProductType ="1"
```

WMI query for Windows 8:

```
SELECT * FROM Win32_OperatingSystem WHERE Version LIKE "6.2%" AND
ProductType ="1"
```

Basically, the version is the OS version, and the ProductType=1 means that it is a client operating system.

Create and Apply a WMI Filter

1. On **CL01**, log in as **Administrator** in the **VIAMONSTRA** domain.

2. Start the **Group Policy Management** console.

3. In the left pane, right-click **WMI Filters** and select **New**.

4. In the **Name** field, enter **Windows 7** and then click **Add**.

5. In the **Query** text area, enter:

```
SELECT * FROM Win32_OperatingSystem WHERE Version LIKE "6.1%" AND
ProductType ="1"
```

6. Click **OK** and then click **Save**.

7. Right-click **WMI Filters** again and select **New**.

8. In the **Name** field, enter **Windows 8** and then click **Add**.

9. In the **Query** text area, enter:

```
SELECT * FROM Win32_OperatingSystem WHERE Version LIKE "6.2%" AND
ProductType ="1"
```

10. Click **OK** and then click **Save**. Do not close the **Group Policy Management** console.

11. Expand the **User Accounts** OU, and select the **User Configuration** GPO.

12. Make sure that the **Scope** tab is the active one, and at the very bottom of the page, click the drop-down list under **WMI Filtering**.

13. Choose **Windows 7**, and when asked **Would you like to change the WMI filter to Windows 7?**, click **Yes**.

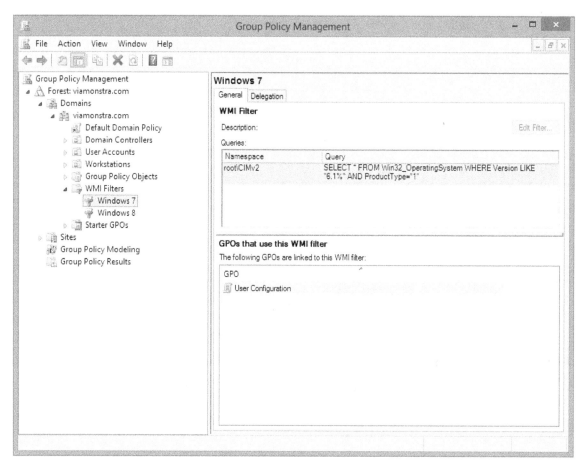

A WMI filter used to apply a GPO depending on which OS the user is logging in to.

Verify That WMI Filtering Is in Place

1. On **CL01**, log in as **Don** in the **VIAMONSTRA** domain.

2. Start a **command prompt**, type the following command, and press **Enter**:

   gpupdate

3. Start a **command prompt**, type the following command, and press **Enter**:

   gpresult /r

Note what it says under **The following GPOs were not applied because they were filtered out**. The User Configuration GPO is filtered out because it has the target WMI filter set for being applied only on Windows 7 machines.

4. Before finishing this lab, you need to set the WMI filter to be used to **None** for the GPO named **User Configuration** so that subsequent labs work properly.

> **Note**: Changing the WMI filter to the Windows 8 WMI filter has the effect that the GPO will be applied only when the targeted user logs in to a Windows 8 machine.

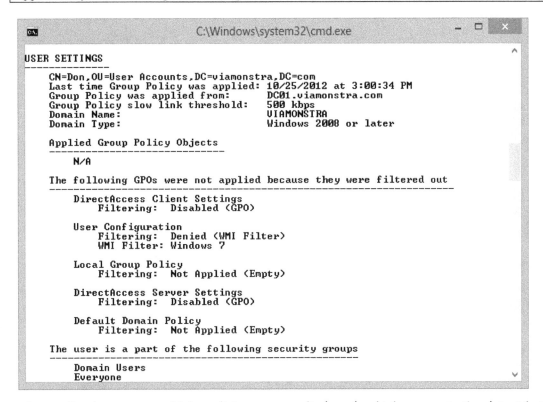

Gpresult shows you which policies are applied and which are not (and in that case also why).

Loopback Processing

Loopback processing simply means that you apply user settings to computer machines, and the user settings are located in the same place the machines are. A prerequisite for using loopback processing is that you keep computers in separate OUs—for instance, XP computer accounts in one OU and Windows 8 computer accounts in another OU.

You then create GPO objects in the OU for Windows 8 and configure the user setting in group policies there, as well. You should always separate Computer and User Configuration in the GPOs.

153

Activate Loopback Processing Mode

1. On **DC01**, log in as **Administrator** in the **VIAMONSTRA** domain.

2. Using the **Group Policy Management** console, edit the **Workstation Configuration** group policy.

3. In the **Computer Configuration** / **Policies** / **Administrative Templates** / **System** / **Group Policy** node, configure the following:

   > Enable the **Configure user Group Policy loopback processing mode** policy, and set the **Mode** to **Replace**.

Note: If you choose merge mode, all settings that normally would hit your user are merged with the ones you set in this policy. When using replace, you make sure that only the user settings you specify for machines in this particular OU are applied.

---

4. In the **User Configuration** / **Policies** / **Administrative Templates** / **Windows Components** / **File Explorer** node, configure the following:

   > Enable the **Start File Explorer with ribbon minimized** policy. Configure the setting to **Never open new File Explorer windows with the ribbon minimized**.

Verify Loopback Processing Configuration

1. On **CL01**, log in as **John** in the **VIAMONSTRA** domain.

2. Start **File Explorer** and verify that the ribbon interface is displayed.

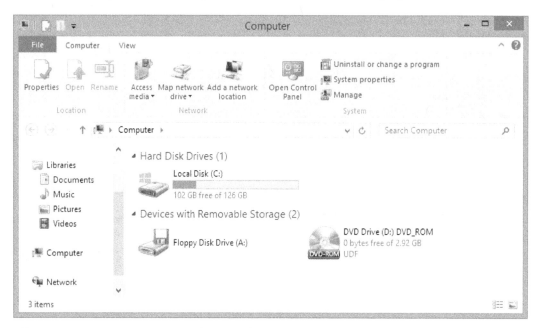

The ribbon interface being displayed.

PowerShell

The traditional distinction between an IT professional and a developer is blurring more and more as scripting and coding increasingly become a part of IT pros' everyday work.

In Windows 8, there is a vast number of PowerShell cmdlets that you can use to customize, manage, and automate things. There are approximately 1300 PowerShell cmdlets in Windows 8. One change from previous Windows versions is that all modules are now loaded by default. You no longer have to import a module for managing AppLocker, for instance, to be able to use those cmdlets. Instead, you have them all available right from the start, which makes everything smoother.

Why PowerShell? Simply because you can automate things in a standardized fashion, you have the support inbox, and there is a PowerShell Integrated Scripting Environment editor that you can use to build your PowerShell solutions.

For a consultant, PowerShell might be a really good solution for automating things; for internal IT departments, it can be used to save time doing standard tasks, such as creating new user accounts, folders, security groups, and so forth.

Find All Module and Cmdlets

1. On **CL01**, log in as **Administrator** in the **VIAMONSTRA** domain.

2. Using the **Start screen**, start **Windows PowerShell** (which starts a PowerShell command prompt).

3. To list all available modules and some of their cmdlets, type the following command and press **Enter**:

   Get-Module –ListAvailable

Now you see a list of all available modules which in turn consist of a number of cmdlets.

A large number of PowerShell cmdlets are included with Windows 8.

Use PowerShell ISE

1. On **CL01**, log in as **Administrator** in the **VIAMONSTRA** domain.

2. Using the **Start screen**, start **Windows PowerShell ISE** to launch the **PowerShell Integrated Scripting Environment (ISE)**.

3. In the **Commands** menu on the right, scroll in the command list, click **New-GPO**, and then click **Show details**.

4. In the **Name** field, enter **New GPO** and click the **Insert** button.

5. Click anywhere in the script window to the left and press the **Enter** key to execute the command. You instantly get feedback that it succeeded and the result is a new domain group policy.

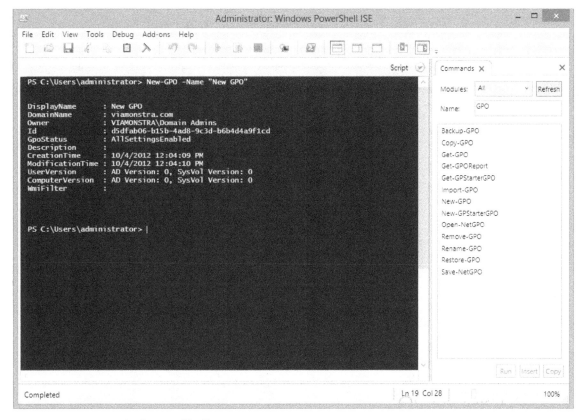

Automating with PowerShell is quite easy.

For Your (PowerShell) Safety

When working with PowerShell, there is one thing you should be aware of and always apply, and that is the safety hatch for escaping from something you did not anticipate. Trust me, bad things can happen.

The safety hatch is called "WhatIf." If you append it to the PowerShell command you are about to run, it presents what will happen if you run the command without the WhatIf switch.

Use the WhatIf Switch

1. On **CL01**, log in as **Administrator** in the **VIAMONSTRA** domain.

2. Using the **Start screen**, start **Windows PowerShell**.

3. Type the following command and press **Enter**:

   Del C:\Windows*.exe –WhatIf

   A list of all of all EXE files that would be deleted with this command are now displayed, and you have a preview of what the command would achieve if run without the WhatIf switch.

```
                              Windows PowerShell                          –  □  ×
PS C:\Users\administrator.DEMO> del C:\Windows\*.exe -WhatIf
What if: Performing operation "Remove file" on Target "C:\Windows\bfsvc.exe".
What if: Performing operation "Remove file" on Target "C:\Windows\explorer.exe".
What if: Performing operation "Remove file" on Target "C:\Windows\HelpPane.exe".
What if: Performing operation "Remove file" on Target "C:\Windows\hh.exe".
What if: Performing operation "Remove file" on Target "C:\Windows\notepad.exe".
What if: Performing operation "Remove file" on Target "C:\Windows\regedit.exe".
What if: Performing operation "Remove file" on Target "C:\Windows\splwow64.exe".
What if: Performing operation "Remove file" on Target "C:\Windows\winhlp32.exe".
What if: Performing operation "Remove file" on Target "C:\Windows\write.exe".
PS C:\Users\administrator.DEMO> _
```

It is always good to use the WhatIf switch before actually executing a command.

Execution Policy

By default on a Windows 8 machine, running PowerShell code is restricted to what is shipped with the operating system. To be able to run PowerShell scripts from other sources, you need to change the execution policy. Setting it to unrestricted will get you going, but I strongly recommend that you set it to run only scripts that are signed. Use the command "Set-ExecutionPolicy Unrestricted" or "Set-ExecutionPolicy AllSigned".

Set the Execution Policy Centrally

1. On **DC01**, log in as **Administrator** in the **VIAMONSTRA** domain.

2. Using the **Group Policy Management** console, edit the **Workstation Configuration** group policy.

3. In the **Computer Configuration** / **Policies** / **Administrative Templates** / **Windows Components** / **Windows PowerShell** node, configure the following:

    Enable the **Turn on Script Execution** policy; then choose the execution policy that fits your organization in terms of security and policy.

Chapter 8

Troubleshooting and Recovery

Regardless of how well Windows 8 operates, you will bump into problems of various kinds. This chapter deals with how to troubleshoot and do recovery when a problem actually occurs. In this chapter, you learn about the new Task Manager, a few points about performance, and how to monitor and troubleshoot using built-in tools such as Windows Resource Monitor and Windows Reliability Monitor.

Task Manager

One of the things in the new Task Manger that appeals to me is a great overview that visually makes it a lot easier to see in real time what is happening on the machine, as well as let you control startup items easily. It is the first time in many years that the Task Manager has had some really nice improvements. The introduction of modern-style apps has contributed to the need to modernize the Task Manager, and the changes are all good.

The Process tab provides the great overview and gives real-time information on each started app or process in terms of CPU, memory, disk, and network utilization.

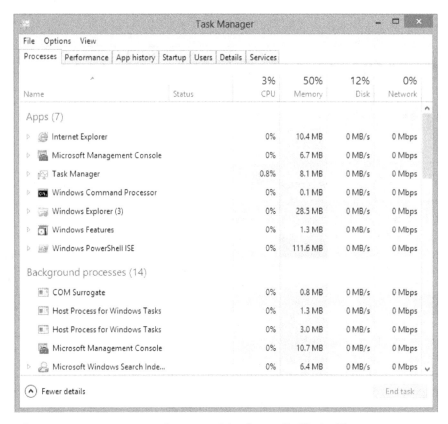

A great overview in the new Windows 8 Task Manager.

Note: If you select any process in Task Manager, it will show an End Task button. However, if you select File Explorer, the button's name and function change to Restart. That is a small but useful new feature.

Controlling Startup Items in Task Manager

The Task Manager in Windows 8 sports not only integration and a listing of which applications are starting along with Windows, but it also shows a rating of the impact they have on startup performance.

How to Check Performance Impact of Startup Items

1. On **CL01**, log in as **Don** in the **VIAMONSTRA** domain.

2. Start **Task Manager** by pressing **Ctrl + Shift + Esc**.

3. If necessary, click **More details** to see Task Manager in its full view.

4. Go to the **Startup** tab.

5. Note all startup applications and specifically note the column **Startup impact**.

6.   Select any item that you want to get rid of to improve the performance of your machine and click **Disable**.

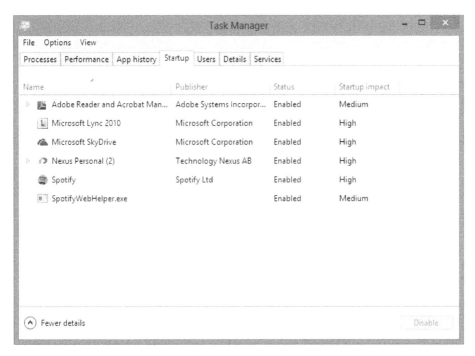

As you can see some startup applications affect performance more than others. Keeping this list short is essential.

Note: Handling the startup items in msonfig.exe is no longer possible as that has been moved entirely to the Task Manager in Windows 8.

Performance

A lot has been done in Windows 8 to further improve performance of the operating system compared to its predecessor Windows 7. Here is a summary of a few things that will make a difference when it comes to performance in Windows 8:

- **Fewer services running**. If you take a quick look in the good old Services.msc console, you will find that a number of services now have a totally new startup mode, Manual (trigger start), and also Automatic (trigger start). This means, for instance, that GPUpdate and Windows Update services are not running all the time but only when you run gpupdate, for example, or start the Windows Update console. Of course, these services wake up from time to time when group policies are refreshed and when automated checking for updates is done.

- **Memory optimizations**. A couple of things have been done to further improve performance, and they have to do with memory handling. To start with, memory combining is being used, which is a sort of memory de-duplication. That means that memory with identical content is reserved only once regardless of the number of pages allocated. Second, Windows 8 introduces the ability for applications and Windows to prioritize memory access as applications can request to use low-priority memory. These are small changes, but ones that nevertheless do optimize memory handling in Windows 8.

- **Web browser and graphics performance**. Both Internet Explorer and the graphics subsystem have undergone major changes to provide a really good platform for modern Windows 8 applications, as well as HTML5 web applications.

- **Much more**. There are more performance improvements done in Windows 8, such as energy optimizations that make your laptop batteries last longer.

The following table charts a performance comparison of a freshly installed Windows 7 versus Windows 8.

Metric	Windows 7 Enterprise x64	Windows 8 Enterprise x64
Number of processes	33	27
Memory	460	403
Installation	7:54 (min:sec)	6:11 (min:sec)
Startup time	0:46 (min:sec)	0:37 (min:sec)
Browser mark	39682 (Internet Explorer 9)	150239 (Internet Explorer 10)

Note: For all the values other than browser mark, lower is better. For browser mark, a higher value is better. The tests were performed on clean installations of both Windows versions, restarting the machines four times, and the values were measured after the machine had been running for 10 minutes. The conclusion is that Windows 8 has a significant performance increase compared to Windows 7.

Push-Button Reset

Another new feature in Windows 8 goes by the name **push-button reset**. It really not just one feature, it contain two mechanisms: either resetting the machine (Reset your PC) or just refreshing the machine (Refresh your PC).

The concept of push-button reset is that you have an image on the local drive of a machine. You can then, with the click of a button, either completely restore the machine to the original image, wiping all settings and files, or you can choose to refresh the machine and keep settings and files.

The feature is primarily intended for OEMs creating recovery media that will be more dynamic than just wiping everything to factory defaults. There are uses for this in enterprises, as well, as you might have users who are very mobile or do not come to the office very often. For them, the possibility of doing a refresh can be essential for getting rid of certain problems.

Reset Your PC

Reset your PC means that you restore the operating system to the state of the image that you placed on the local drive. During a reset, all local settings and files are lost (unless you are using roaming user profiles, folder redirection, or UE-V).

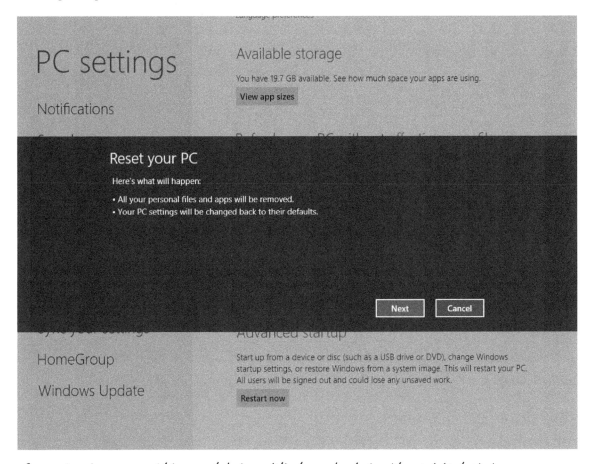

A reset wipes everything and brings Windows back to the original state.

Refresh Your PC

Refresh your PC is just like a reset except that all settings and files are restored. The mechanism behind the scene is the User State Migration Tool (USMT), which is commonly used in Windows deployments that involve "refresh" installs.

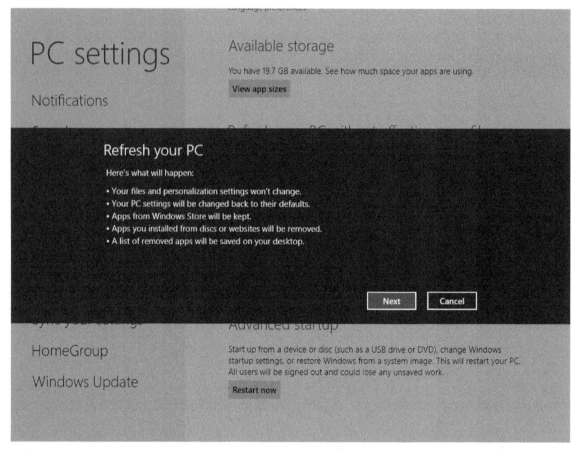

When doing a refresh of your PC, files and settings are retained.

Stage Push-Button Reset

In these steps, I assume you have a Windows 8 ISO.

1. On **CL02**, log in as **Administrator** in the **VIAMONSTRA** domain.

2. Mount the **Windows 8** ISO file.

3. Using **File Explorer**, create a folder called **RecoveryImage** in the root of the **C:** drive.

4. Using **File Explorer**, navigate to **D:\sources**, and copy the **install.wim** file to **C:\RecoveryImage**.

5. Start an elevated **command prompt** (run as administrator), type the following command, and press **Enter**:

   ReAgentc /setosimage /path C:\RecoveryImage\install.wim /index 1 /target C:\Windows

Real World Note: In a real-world scenario, you most likely use the image which you have custom made, the so-called reference image.

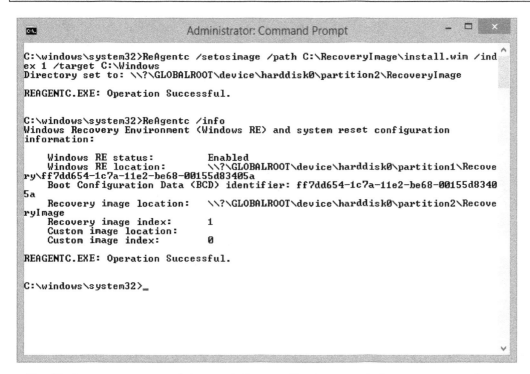

The ReAgentc command is used for configuring push-button reset features.

Refresh a Machine

1. On **CL02**, log in as **Administrator** in the **VIAMONSTRA** domain.

2. Press the **Windows logo key + C** to bring up the **charms**, click **Settings**, and then click **Change PC settings** (available in the lower right-hand corner).

3. Click the **General** tab and then scroll down to find the reset and refresh options (the refresh option is named **Refresh your PC without affecting your files** and the reset option is named **Remove everything and reinstall Windows**).

4. Under **Refresh your PC without affecting your files**, click **Get started**.

5. When the **Refresh your PC** message appears, take note of what will happen, and then click **Next**.

6. When the **Ready to refresh your PC** message appears, click **Refresh** to let the refresh begin.

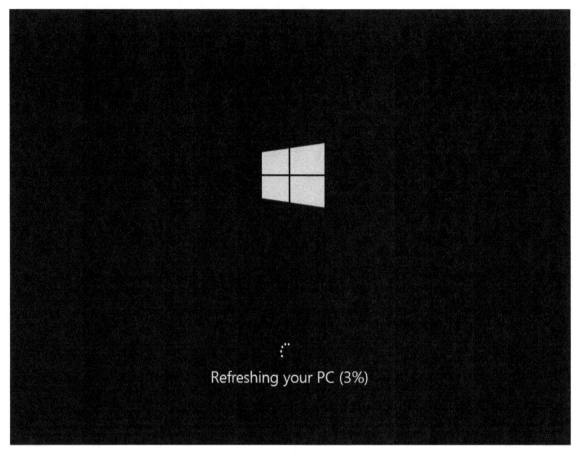

Refreshing your PC (3%)

Refreshing your PC will take some time to finish.

Windows Resource Monitor

A few years ago you had little chance of quickly finding out what was hogging your system resources when it became really slow, or if you noticed that the hard drive was spinning like crazy doing "something." In Windows 8, you have a nice little utility that will help you in these scenarios: Windows Resource Monitor.

The thing about Windows Resource Monitor is that it lists whatever is going on in terms of CPU, memory, disk, and network. Those four categories are where bottlenecks form that affect performance in a machine.

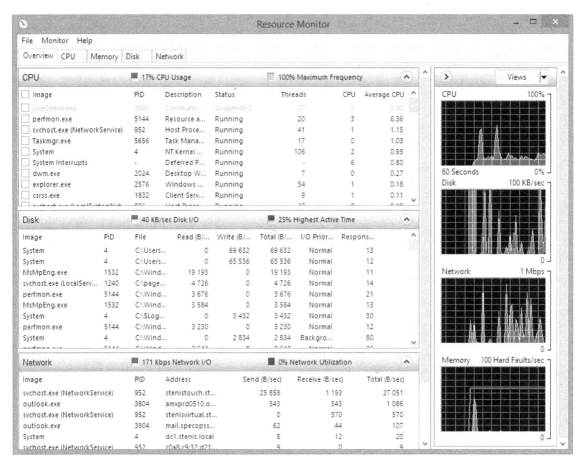

The Overview tab in Resource Monitor gives you basic information, and you can drill down and gain more information on what is happening on the machine in question.

At first glance, Windows Resource Monitor seems kind of basic, but if you drill down, you will learn that it is pretty useful and advanced. There are, of course, more advanced third-party tools in the market, but Windows Resource Monitor often will get you far enough.

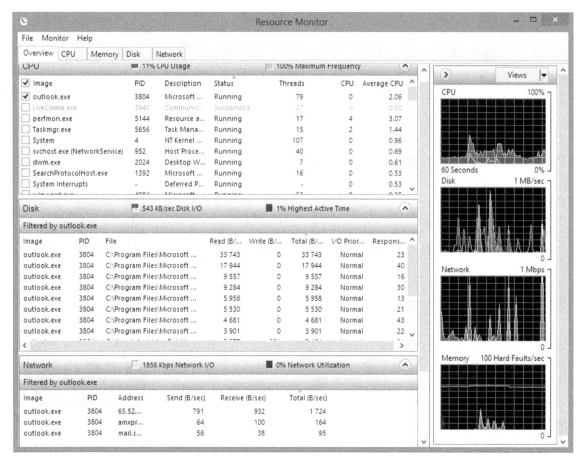

Here you can see how the Outlook·exe process is filtered for that process only, and as you can see in the graph to the right, it shows Outlook specifics related to the overall performance·

Real World Note: I use this tool all the time to see what is going on in a system. For instance, I can check and see what is happening on a distribution point for ConfigMgr or on Hyper-V servers to find out what is currently hogging the machine's resources.

Find Out What Is Happening on a Machine

1. On **CL01**, log in as **Administrator** in the **VIAMONSTRA** domain.

2. Go to the **desktop**, right-click the **taskbar**, and choose **Task Manager**.

3. Click the **Performance** tab, followed by a click on the link **Open Resource Monitor**.

Note: A much quicker way of starting Resource Monitor is to start it from the Start screen, or via Run (Windows logo key + R) by typing perfmon /res.

4. In **Resource Monitor**, explore the various tabs and the information.

5. When done, close **Resource Monitor**.

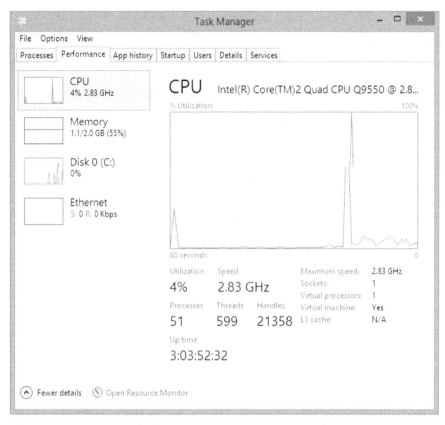

Task Manager in Windows 8 gives an improved view over performance compared to Windows 7 and previous Windows versions.

Windows Reliability Monitor

Ever since Windows Vista was released, there has been a somewhat hidden feature in Windows, called Windows Reliability Monitor. This tool gathers information about common events and problems that occur on your machine, such as the following:

- **Installations and uninstallations**. Applications and drivers that are installed or uninstalled are listed, as are applications that are upgraded.

- **Crashes**. If an application, service, driver, or Windows itself crashes, it will be listed in Windows Reliability Monitor.

- **Windows Update**. Patched or drivers that are installed via Windows Update are listed, as are errors with installing updates or drivers from Windows Update.

171

Really Useful When Troubleshooting

Simply put, the fewer problems that occur on your machine, the higher the rating on the 10-point index scale. Looking at the events in Windows Reliability Monitor will often help you see patterns and clues of what has happened on the machine, and in the case of problems, when they started.

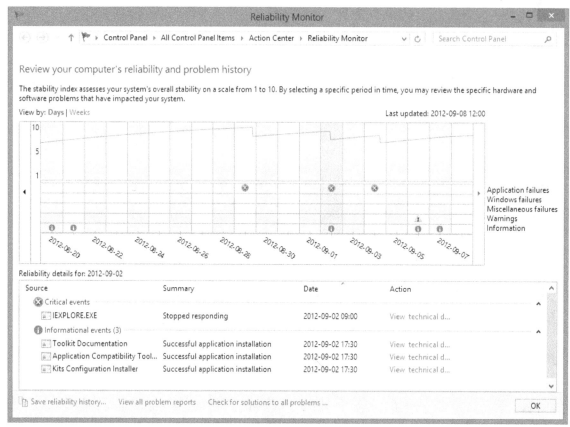

Reliability Monitor is great for seeing exactly what has happened over time on a machine.

Investigate the History and Stability of a Machine

1. On **CL01**, log in as **Don** in the **VIAMONSTRA** domain.

2. Press the **Windows logo key + W**, type **reliability**, and choose **View reliability history**.

3. Review and explore the reliability history and, if necessary, change **View by** to **Weeks** .

4. For a detailed list of all application, driver, and Windows crashes, click the link at the bottom called **View all problem reports**. Note that you also can save the reliability history in XML format by clicking the **Save reliability history** link.

5. When done exploring, close the **Reliability Monitor**.

> **Note**: Unfortunately, you cannot connect to and see the information remotely from another machine like you can with most other MMC consoles. This information needs to be accessed and read locally.

Easy Assessment of Performance Issues

There are great tools that will help you find performance issues on your machines. Windows Performance Toolkit (part of the Windows ADK) is one of them. Among the problems that the tool can find, issues with group policies are often the ones with the most significant performance impact in enterprise environments.

However, something that most people are totally unaware of is that some performance assessment is going on in Windows 8 at all times. The information from that ongoing assessment is something that you can easily take advantage of, particularly when you are troubleshooting a machine.

Find Performance Issues

This lab won't work well on the virtual machine that you are using, so instead perform these steps on a machine that you have been using for a while and, for the best end result, a machine that you have been using in a production environment.

1. Press **Windows logo key + W**, type **performance**, and then open **Performance Information and Tools**.

2. In the left pane, click **Advanced tools**.

3. Under the section **Performance issues**, notice any issues that are listed and click some of them to see what the problems are and possibly how to resolve them.

> **Real World Note**: The kind of information you can get here are things that cause a slow machine startup or shutdown, for instance. I have seen examples where you find that a particular driver is causing a slow sleep and restore from sleep mode. Upgrading that particular driver is likely to fix the problem.

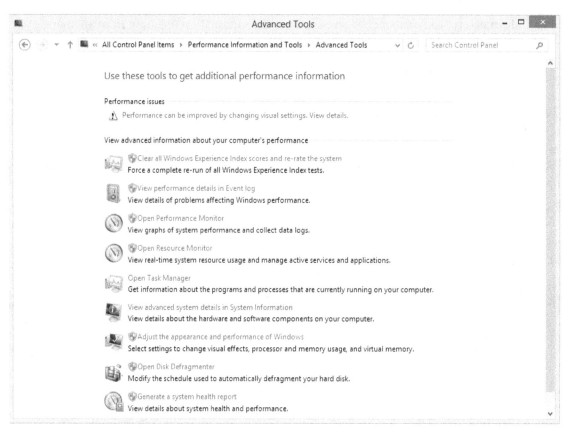

Performance Information and Tools is a quick source for finding performance issues.

Chapter 9

Microsoft Desktop Optimization Pack

Microsoft Desktop Optimization Pack (MDOP) consists of a number of standalone tools and technologies that in more than one way add value to your client platform. It is available for addition to your existing software assurance agreement, but also can be found on TechNet for evaluation purposes.

Overview

The following products are included in MDOP:

- **Advanced Group Policy Management**. A tool that gives Group Policy Management version-control, auditing, and approval mechanisms. A must in an enterprise environment.

- **Application Virtualization**. A tool for packaging ("sequencing") and running applications as virtual applications.

- **Diagnostics and Recovery Toolset**. This is a sort of "rescue disk" used for troubleshooting. It includes a number of tools that help you restore functionality of a malfunctioning machine, or just for recovering a lost administrator password or cleaning a computer of malware.

- **Microsoft BitLocker Administration and Monitoring**. This enables enterprise management of BitLocker, providing status reports and giving helpdesk or end users a self-service portal for obtaining the recovery keys.

- **User Experience Virtualization**. A tool that roams settings between computers.

Previously Microsoft Enterprise Desktop Virtualization (MED-V), System Center Desktop Error Monitoring (SCDEM), and Asset Intelligence System (AIS) were included in MDOP, but they are no longer a part of it in the MDOP 2012 release.

> **Note**: UE-V was covered in full in Chapter 3 and will therefore not be mentioned further in this chapter.

Advanced Group Policy Management (AGPM)

AGPM is one of my favorite tools and is a really important one in enterprise environments. What it does is let you gain complete control over your group policies, control that the regular tools do not provide in any way.

The primary features of AGPM:

- **Version control**. Every change you make to a GPO controlled by AGPM is kept in a change history. It also lets you compare which settings changed at what point in time and enables you to easily roll back a group policy to a previous version.

- **Revision**. You have the option to use multiple roles for group policies, which means you have an approval scheme for changes. For example, if a group policy technician makes a change, it has to be reviewed by a more senior technician before it can be deployed.

The Architecture of AGPM

AGPM consist of two parts: one server installation done on a domain controller and one client that is deployed to all machines for which you manage group policies. When implemented, it displays a new option called Change Control in the Group Policy Management console's left navigation. That is where you then take control over a group policy so it is managed in terms of history, approval schemes, and so forth.

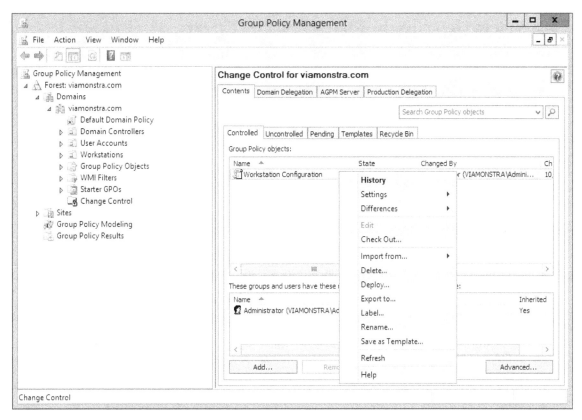

The Group Policy Management console, showing the Change Control option that appears after you install AGPM and is where you manage all GPOs.

Real World Note: I have two things to say about AGPM from my experience. When controlling a GPO in AGPM, remove the edit rights from the GPO's security to make sure that Group Policy technicians cannot edit the GPO the old way in the Group Policy Management console. Also be aware that changes for security filtering and WMI are a bit tricky. To implement such changes, you must make the changes and then do an "Import from production" in AGPM to save them; otherwise, they will be lost when you deploy a GPO.

Application Virtualization (App-V)

App-V has evolved over the years since Microsoft purchased SoftGrid, as it was called back then. App-V provides the means to package an application and deliver it to a Windows machine. The benefits of using App-V when packaging an application is that installing the application will not affect the operating system by adding DLL files and registry entries all over the machine.

Instead, all files are kept in a bubble, where everything runs in isolation. A benefit is that App-V requires little testing, as the application does not integrate itself in the system or affect any other applications on a machine.

Diagnostics and Recovery Toolset (DaRT)

Whenever you encounter a Windows machine that cannot start, what do you do? The reason for a machine not starting Windows properly can be a significant number of things. Among the possible causes are a security update, malware, bad hardware, a bad driver, or that someone forgot the password of the local administrator account.

That is where DaRT comes in. With DaRT, you boot up a machine and have a number of tools that you can use to troubleshoot and fix the malfunctioning machine.

DaRT has a Windows PE image, which is used to boot a machine via a USB memory stick, DVD, or PXE, or from a local DaRT image.

Tools Included in DaRT

The DaRT collection consists of the following tools:

- **Computer Management**. The good old Computer Management console.
- **Crash Analyzer**. A tool that uses Windows Debugging Tools to analyze why the infamous blue screen of death prevents your machine from starting.
- **Defender**. A tool that performs malware scans while the system is offline, which is sometimes the only way to remove some types of malware.
- **Disk Commander and Disk Wipe**. Disk tools that help you recover, repair, or delete disks.
- **Explorer**. File Explorer, does not need further introduction.
- **File Restore**. A tool for recovering deleted files.
- **File Search**. A utility that you can use to search for files on the disk.
- **Hotfix Uninstall**. An uninstall tool for removing patches in cases where a machine is not booting properly due to a Windows security update or hotfix.
- **Locksmith**. A tool that can reset passwords for local accounts.
- **Registry Editor**. The classic Registry Editor that lets you modify registry keys and settings.
- **SFC Scan**. A utility that can run a check to determine whether the system files are all okay and restore them if some are missing or corrupted.
- **TCP Config**. A tool for manually configuring network settings.

Remote Fixing of Problems

Although DaRT is really effective for fixing problems when you have physical access to a machine, it has previously been very hard to do some types of troubleshooting remotely. Starting with DaRT 7.5 (version 8 is included in MDOP 2012), you can either put it on the local hard drive or let the user do a PXE boot, and you can then remote control the DaRT tools. This is very good as you do not have to send a support technician to a computer, or have the user send the computer to you to get it fixed.

You can activate an option so that the remote connection is initiated automatically when booting DaRT. That way, you can connect, enter the administrator credentials, and then start troubleshooting and fixing whatever the problem is. You can find more about how to configure automatic remote connection at http://bit.ly/tlqkOI (reads lowercase T, L, Q and K followed by capital O and I).

> **Real World Note**: If you have pre-staged your machines with DaRT, you are required to enter the credentials of a local administrator account to get into DaRT and start troubleshooting and fixing a problem. This is sometimes an obstacle to using DaRT because many enterprises do not have any local administrator accounts.

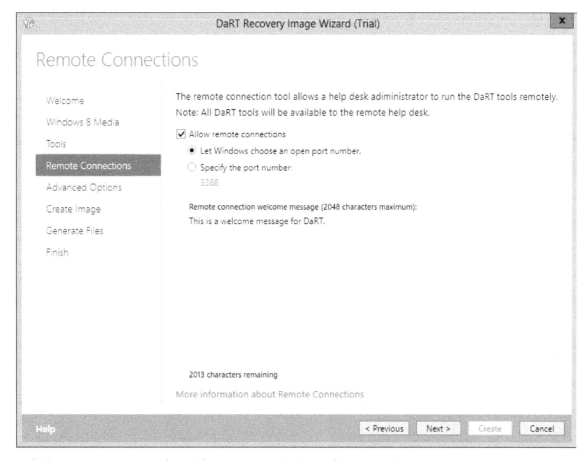

While customizing and building your DaRT media, you also can configure remote connections.

Microsoft BitLocker Administration and Monitoring (MBAM)

If you are running BitLocker, there are a few challenges out there that you cannot solve with the built-in configuration in Windows 8. The benefits of using MBAM are that you get full status information and reporting so you can see which machines are encrypted. In a normal BitLocker deployment, you can force the encryption during deployment, but there is no way to verify the status or enforce BitLocker encryption on machines.

One of the concerns with BitLocker is that once you hand out the recovery key to a remote user who is having problems booting the machine, you cannot reset the recovery key. That means the user may write it down because it contains 48 digits. With MBAM, the recovery key is automatically reset after you have unlocked a machine.

In the traditional BitLocker scenario, you save the recovery keys to Active Directory; but in MBAM, you save them to a SQL Server database.

> **Note**: The SQL database hosting the recovery keys must be an enterprise or datacenter edition of SQL Server because transparent data encryption feature is required. That is required for adding maximum protection for the recovery keys.

Starting with the MDOP 2012 release of MBAM, there is a self-service portal where users can recover their own keys, without having to contact helpdesk or support at all. Additionally, MBAM now can be integrated into System Center Configuration Manager for complete control over it.

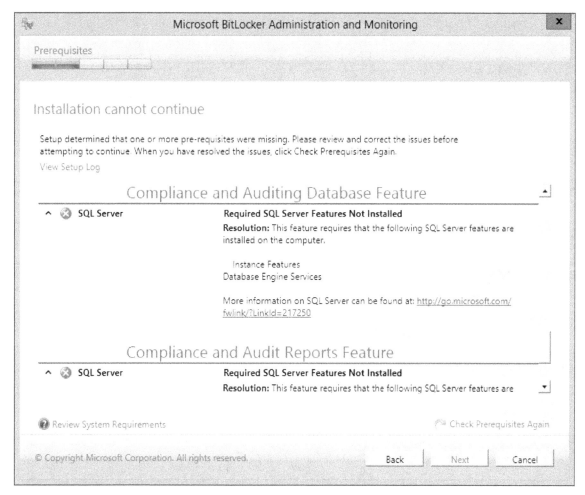

MBAM does have a few pre-requirements that must be in place before installation of all the roles can proceed.

Features of MBAM

There are a number of reasons why you should be using MBAM in an enterprise environment if you are using BitLocker on your machines:

- **Automation**. It is possible to encrypt machines automatically with BitLocker during a new deployment or for machines already running. The MBAM agent, in combination with group policies, handles the encryption on the clients.

- **Compliance and reporting**. You can pull reports and compliance data from MBAM, which gives you a good overview on the status of machines using BitLocker.

- **Self-service**. When a machine enters recovery mode, the user needs the 48-digit recovery password to unlock the machine and proceed booting into Windows. The user can get the recovery password from a web site, rather than having to call helpdesk.

181

- **Security**. Overall security is better when using MBAM than using a traditional BitLocker deployment. A PIN requirement to skip easy PIN codes is one feature. Having complete control over BitLocker and the status is also something important from a security standpoint.

- **System Center Configuration Manager integration**. You can integrate MBAM into System Center Configuration Manager if you are using that tool to manage your Windows clients.

Appendix A
Lab Environment

In this appendix, you find detailed steps to build an exact copy of the lab environment used for the step-by-step guides in this book. To help you create the environment quickly and easily, you find a ready-made hydration kit (an automated setup) in the book sample files, but you also find manual steps in this appendix if you prefer to do everything manually.

The lab environment in this book runs on virtual machines, and the sample files have been tested on the following virtual platforms:

- Hyper-V in Windows 8

- Hyper-V in Windows Server 2012

But before deploying the virtual machine, either automated or manually, you need to download some software for the various labs.

Real World Note: The lab environment is exactly what the name implies: a lab environment so you can follow the step-by-step guides in this book. For a production environment, you need at least one additional domain controller and a dedicated fileserver for the WDS, MDT, MAP, and ACT components.

Preparing Tools for the Labs
In the step-by-step guides in this book, you find references to a Tools.iso file, which includes software needed for the guides. This is where you create that file.

Download the Mandatory Tools for the Labs

1. On the machine (client or server) that you use to manage Hyper-V, create the **C:\Tools** folder.

2. Download the following tools to the **C:\Tools** folder on the host machine:

   - **Assessment and Deployment Kit (ADK)**

   - **Application Verifier 4.0**

   - **Coreinfo (extract the Coreinfo.zip file)**

   - **Microsoft Assessment and Planning (MAP) Toolkit 7.0**

   - **MDT 2012 Update 1**

   - **Remote Server Administration Tools (RSAT) for Windows 8**

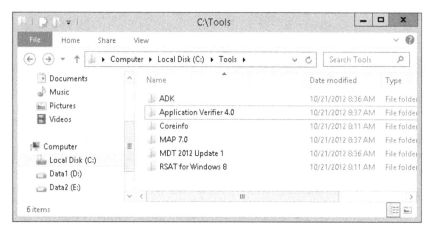

The C:\Tools folder containing the mandatory software.

Download the Optional Tools for the Labs

If you do have access to Microsoft Desktop Optimization Pack (MDOP) 2012, you also can add the tools that will be used in the User Experience Virtualization labs.

1. On the machine (client or server) that you use to manage Hyper-V, in the **C:\Tools** folder, create the **User Experience Virtualization** folder.

2. From the MDOP 2012 ISO, from the **UE-V\Installers\x64** folder, copy the content to the folder you created in step 1:

    User Experience Virtualization

Create the ISO

To create the ISO, you use the oscdimg tool, which is included with ADK.

1. On the machine (client or server) that you use to manage Hyper-V, install **ADK** (**C:\Tools\ADK\adksetup.exe**) and select to install only the following features (clear the other check boxes):

    o   **Deployment Tools**

    o   **Windows Preinstallation Environment (Windows PE)**

> **Note:** The Windows Preinstallation Environment (Windows PE) feature is needed only if you use the hydration kit later in this appendix to build the lab environment. If you decide on going the manual route, you can skip that feature.

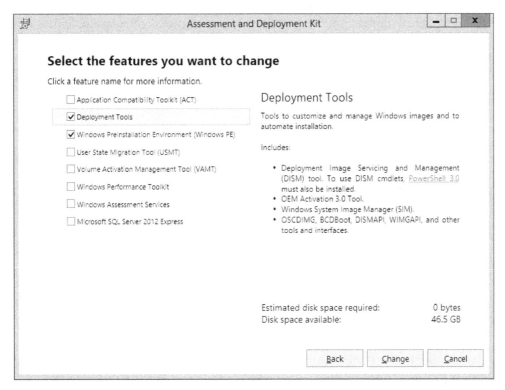

The ADK Setup wizard.

2. Using **File Explorer**, create the **C:\ISO** folder.

3. Start a **Deployment and Imaging Tools Environment** command prompt (found on the Start screen).

4. In the **Deployment and Imaging Tools Environment** command prompt, type the following command and press **Enter**:

    oscdimg -u2 C:\Tools C:\ISO\Tools.iso

    Wait for the ISO to be created in the **C:\ISO** folder.

Virtual Machines: Automated Setup

Again, to deploy the virtual machines for lab environment you have two options: you can use the hydration kit provided in the book sample files to do an automated setup, or you can skip this section and follow the manual steps provided in the section "Deploying the Virtual Machines: Manual Setup" later in this appendix.

If you still are reading this section, I assume you are interested in the automated setup. ☺

The automated setup, the hydration kit, that you download as part of the book sample files is just a folder structure and some scripts. The scripts help you create MDT 2012 Update 1 Lite Touch offline media, and the folder structure is there for you to add your downloaded software media when applicable. You also can use trial versions for the lab software. The overview steps are the following:

- Download additional software
- Extract the hydration kit and prepare the deployment share
- Populate the hydration folder structure with setup media
- Generate the hydration media item (ISO file)
- Create two virtual machines and deploy them from the hydration media item

Preparing the Hydration Environment

You need to have local administrator rights/permissions on the Windows machine that you use to manage Hyper-V.

You also need to have at least 30 GB of free disk space on C:\ for the hydration kit and at least 100 GB of free space for the volume hosting your virtual machines. Also make sure to run all commands from an elevated command prompt.

These steps should be performed on the machine that you use to manage Hyper-V.

Download the Additional Software

1. On the Windows machine that you use to manage Hyper-V, verify that you have at least 30 GB of free disk space.

2. Download the following software to the **C:\Tools** folder:

    o   **Windows Server 2012 Standard or Datacenter (trial or full version)**

    o   **Windows 8 Enterprise x64 (trial or full version)**

    o   **Sysinternals BGInfo**

    o   **The book sample files (extract to C:\Tools)**

Real World Note: BGInfo also can be copied from the MDT 2012 Update 1 installation directory. Microsoft included the x86 and x64 versions of BGInfo in MDT 2012 Update 1.

Create the Hydration Deployment Share

1. On the Windows machine that you use to manage Hyper-V, install **MDT 2012 Update 1** (**MicrosoftDeploymentToolkit2012_x64.msi**) with the default settings.

2. From the book sample files, copy the **HydrationW8** folder to **C:**.

3. You should now have the following folder containing a few subfolders and PowerShell scripts:

    C:\\HydrationW8\\Source

4. In an elevated (run as administrator) **PowerShell command prompt**, configure Execution Policy in PowerShell by running the following command:

    Set-ExecutionPolicy Unrestricted -Force

5. In the **PowerShell command prompt**, navigate to the hydration folder by running the following command:

    Set-Location C:\\HydrationW8\\Source

6. Still in **PowerShell command prompt**, with location (working directory) set to **C:\\HydrationW8\\Source**, create the hydration deployment share by running the following command:

    .\\1_CreateHydrationDeploymentShare.ps1

7. Merge the hydration kit content with the new deployment share by running the following command:

    .\\2_MergeDeploymentShareWithHydrationKit.ps1

Populate the Hydration Deployment Share with the Setup Files

1. Copy the **ADK** installation files the following folder:

    C:\\HydrationW8\\DS\\Applications\\Install - ADK\\Source

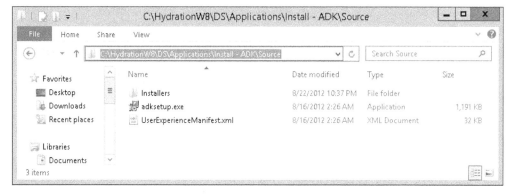

The ADK installation files copied·

2. Copy the **BGInfo** file (**bginfo.exe**) to the following folder:

   C:\HydrationW8\DS\Applications\Install - BGInfo\Source

3. Copy the **MDT 2012 Update 1** installation file
   (**MicrosoftDeploymentToolkit2012_x64.msi**) to the following folder:

   C:\HydrationW8\DS\Applications\Install - MDT 2012 Update 1\Source

4. Copy the **Windows Server 2012** installation files (the content of the ISO, not the actual ISO) to the following folder:

   C:\HydrationW8\DS\Operating Systems\Windows Server 2012

5. Copy the **Windows 8 Enterprise x64** installation files (again, the content of the ISO, not the actual ISO) to the following folder:

   C:\HydrationW8\DS\Operating Systems\Windows 8 Enterprise x64

Create the Hydration ISO (MDT 2012 Update Offline Media Item)

1. Using **Deployment Workbench** (available on the Start screen), expand **Deployment Shares**, and expand **Hydration W8**.

2. Review the various nodes. The **Operating Systems** and **Task Sequences** nodes should both have content in them.

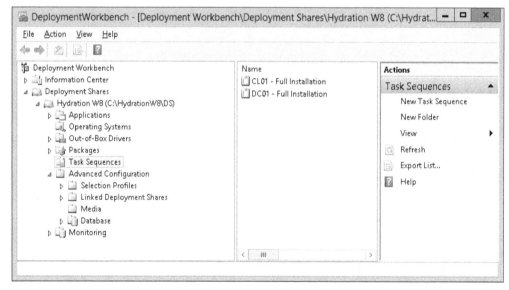

The Hydration W8 deployment share, listing all task sequences.

3. Expand the **Advanced Configuration** node, and then select the **Media** node.

4. In the right pane, right-click the **MEDIA001** item, and select **Update Media Content**.

Note: The media update will take a while to run, a perfect time for a coffee break. ☺

After the media update is complete, you will have a large ISO (**HydrationW8.iso**) in the **C:\HydrationW8\ISO** folder. The HydrationW8.iso will be about 9 GB in size.

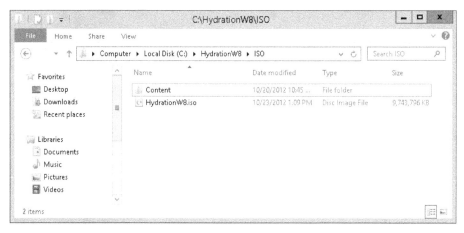

The HydrationW8·iso media item·

Start the Automated Setup
In these steps, you deploy and configure the virtual machines for the lab environment.

Deploy DC01
This is the primary domain controller used in the environment, and it also is running DNS and DHCP.

1. Using **Hyper-V Manager**, create a virtual machine with the following settings:

   a. Name: **DC01**

   b. Hard drive: **127 GB** (dynamic disk)

   c. Memory: **2 GB**

   d. Network: The virtual network for the lab environment

   e. Image file (ISO): **C:\HydrationW8\ISO\HydrationW8.iso**

2. Start the **DC01** virtual machine. After booting from **HydrationW8.iso**, and after WinPE has loaded, select the **DC01** task sequence.

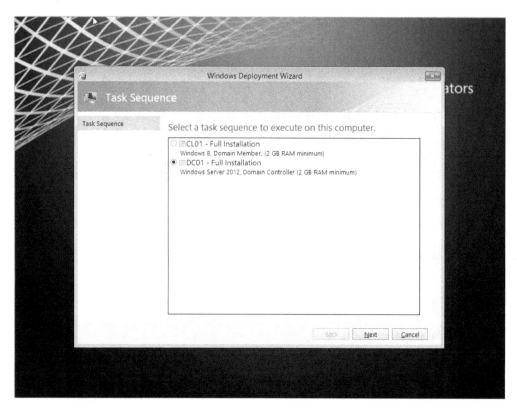

The list of hydration task sequences.

Wait until the setup is complete and you see the **Hydration Complete** message in the final summary.

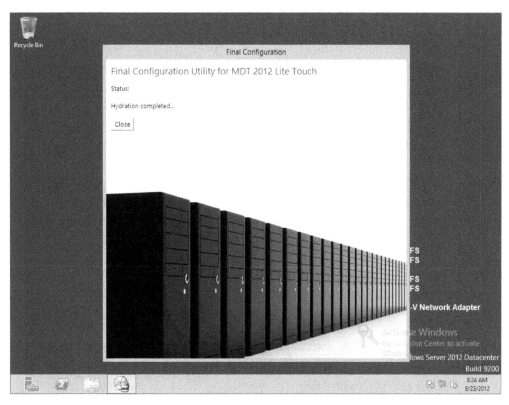

The deployment of DC01 completed, showing the custom final summary screen·

Deploy CL01

After DC01 has been deployed, you can deploy the CL01 Windows 8 Enterprise client. Make sure that DC01 is running when you deploy the CL01 client.

1. Using **Hyper-V Manager**, create a virtual machine with the following settings:

    a. Name: **CL01**

    b. Hard drive: **127 GB** (dynamic disk)

    c. Memory: **2 GB**

    d. Network: The virtual network for the lab environment

    e. Image file (ISO): **C:\HydrationW8\ISO\HydrationW8.iso**

2. Start the **CL01** virtual machine. After booting from **HydrationW8.iso**, and after WinPE has loaded, select the **CL01** task sequence.

    Wait until the setup is complete and you see the **Hydration Complete** message in the final summary.

Virtual Machines: Manual Setup

The hydration kit configures the virtual machines with all the settings required for the other step-by-step guides in this book. If you want to do all this manually instead of the automated setup provided, this section covers the necessary configuration.

> **Note:** These steps are not needed if you deployed the virtual machines using the hydration kit provided in the book sample files.

DC01 Configuration

In these steps, I assume you have a virtual machine named DC01 with a default setup of Windows Server 2012 Standard or Datacenter edition installed to a single 127 GB partition and 2 GB of RAM.

Network Configuration

1. On the **DC01** virtual machine, log in as a local **Administrator**.

2. Set the computer name to **DC01** and reboot when prompted.

3. After rebooting, log in again, start **ncpa.cpl**, and choose **Properties** for the network card. Set the following **IP configuration** for TCP/IP v4 settings:

    a. IP address: **192.168.0.100**

    b. Subnet mask: **255.255.255.0**

    c. DNS: **192.168.0.100**

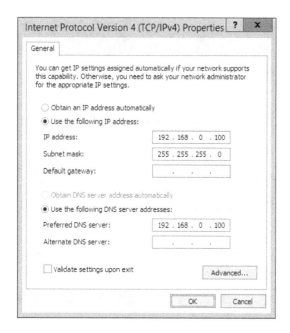

DCO1 network configuration·

Configure Active Directory Domain Services (ADDS)

1. Set the password for the local **Administrator** account to **Pa$$w0rd**.
2. Using **Server Manager**, click **Add roles and features**.
3. If the **Before you begin** page is displayed, select the **Skip this page by default** check box and click **Next**.
4. On the **Select installation type** page, select **Role-based or feature-based installation**.
5. On the **Select destination server** page, select **DC01** and click **Next**.
6. On the **Select server roles** page, select the **Active Directory Domain Services** role.
7. In the **Add Roles and Features Wizard** dialog box, select **Add Features**, and then click **Next**.
8. On the **Select features** page, accept the default settings and click **Next**.
9. On the **Active Directory Domain Services** page, click **Next**.
10. On the **Confirm installation selections** page, click **Install**.
11. After the installation is completed, on the **Installation progress** page, click the **Promote this server to a domain controller** link.

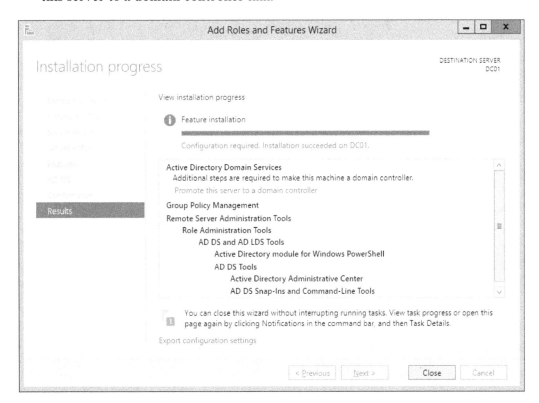

The Installation progress page, displaying the "Promote this server to a domain controller" link.

12. In the **Active Directory Domain Services Configuration Wizard**, on the **Deployment Configuration** page, enter the following information and then click **Next**:

    a. **Add a new forest**

    b. Root domain name: **viamonstra.com**

13. On the **Domain Controller Options** page, enter the following information and then click **Next**:

    DSRM password and confirm password: **Pa$$w0rd**

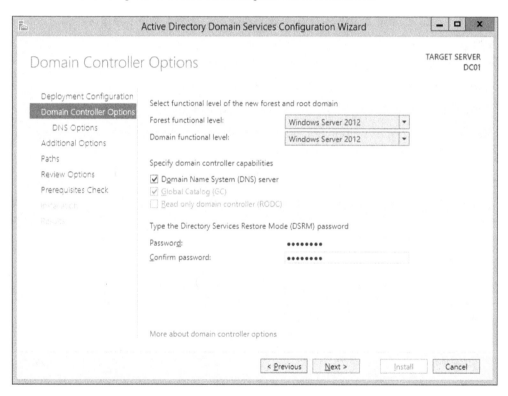

The Domain Controller Options page.

14. On the **DNS Options** page, accept the default settings (ignore the warning about DNS delegation) and click **Next**.

15. On the **Additional Options** page, accept the default settings and click **Next**.

16. On the **Paths** page, accept the default settings and click **Next**.

17. On the **Review Options** page, click **Next**.

18. On the **Prerequisites Check** page, click **Install** and wait for the installation to finish.

Note: DC01 will reboot automatically during install.

Create OUs

1. On **DC01**, log on as **Administrator** in the **VIAMONSTRA** domain.

2. Using **Active Directory Users and Computers**, create the following OUs in the root of **viamonstra.com**:

    a. **Workstations**

    b. **User Accounts**

Create User Accounts

1. Using **Active Directory Users and Computers**, in the **User Accounts** OU, create a **user account** with the following parameters:

    o Username and User logon name: **Don**

    o Password: **Pa$$w0rd**

    o Clear the **User must change password at next logon** check box.

    o Select the **Password never expires** check box.

2. Repeat the preceding step to create another **user account** with the following parameters:

    o Username and User logon name: **John**

    o Password: **Pa$$w0rd**

    o Clear the **User must change password at next logon** check box.

    o Select the **Password never expires** check box.

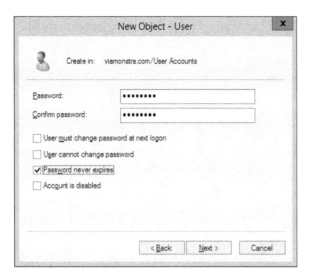

Creating user accounts in Active Directory.

Configure DHCP Role

1. Using **Server Manager**, click **Add roles and features**.

2. On the **Select installation type** page, select **Role-based or feature-based installation**.

3. On the **Select destination server** page, select **DC01** and click **Next**.

4. On the **Select server roles** page, select the **DHCP Server** role.

5. In the **Add Roles and Features Wizard** dialog box, select **Add Features** and then click **Next**.

6. On the **Select features** page, accept the default settings and click **Next**.

7. On the **DHCP Server** page, click **Next**.

8. On the **Confirm installation selections** page, click **Install**.

9. After the installation is completed, on the **Installation progress** page, click the **Complete DHCP configuration** link.

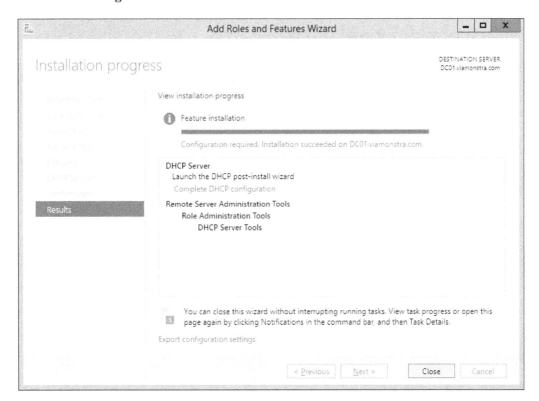

The Installation progress page displaying the Complete DHCP configuration link.

10. In the **DHCP Post-Install configuration wizard**, on the **Description** page, click **Next**.

11. On the **Authorization** page, accept the default settings and click **Commit**.

12. Close the **DHCP Post-Install configuration wizard** and the **Add Roles and Features Wizard**.

13. Using **Server Manager**, select **DHCP** in the left pane, right-click **DC01**, and select **DHCP Manager**.

14. In **DHCP Manager**, expand **DC01.viamonstra.com,** right-click **IPv4** and **select New Scope**.

15. Use the following settings when working through the **New Scope Wizard**:

   a. Scope Name

       Name: **192.168.0.0/24**

   b. IP Address Range

       i. Start IP address: **192.168.0.200**

       ii. End IP address: **192.168.0.250**

       iii. Length: **24**

       iv. Subnet mask: **255.255.255.0**

   c. Add Exclusions and Delay

       <default>

   d. Lease Duration

       <default>

   e. Configure DHCP Options

       Yes, I want to configure these options now

   f. Router (Default Gateway)

       <default>

   g. Domain Name and DNS Servers

       i. Parent domain: **viamonstra.com**

       ii. IP address: **192.168.0.100**

   h. WINS Servers

       <default>

   i. Activate Scope

       Yes, I want to activate this scope now

Install Assessment and Deployment Kit (ADK) on DC01

1. On **DC01**, mount the **Tools.iso** file (located in the C:\ISO folder).

2. Navigate to **D:\ADK** and run **adksetup.exe** to start the installation.

3. On the **Specify location** page, accept the default settings and click **Next**.

4. On the **Join the Customer Experience Improvement Program** page, accept the default settings and click **Next**.

5. On the **Accept License** page, click **Accept**.

6. On the **Select the features you want to install** page, accept the default settings and click **Install**.

7. After the installation is completed, on the **Welcome to the Assessment and Deployment Kit** page, click **Close**.

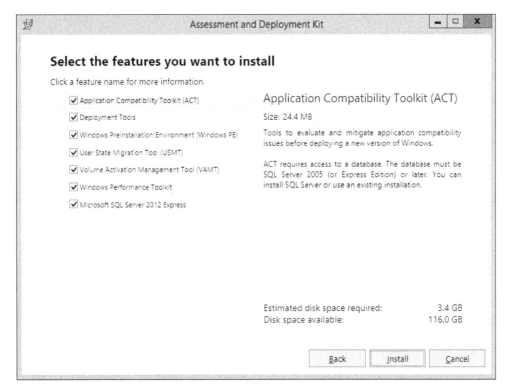

The ADK Setup with default features selected.

Install Windows Deployment Services (WDS)

1. On **DC01**, using **Server Manager**, click **Add roles and features**.

2. On the **Select installation type** page, select **Role-based or feature-based installation**.

3. On the **Select destination server** page, select **DC01.viamonstra.com** and click **Next**.

199

4. On the **Select server roles** page, select the **Windows Deployment Services** role.

5. In the **Add Roles and Features Wizard** dialog box, select **Add Features** and then click **Next**.

6. On the **Select features** page, accept the default settings and click **Next**.

7. On the **WDS** page, click **Next**.

8. On the **Select role services** page, accept the default settings and click **Next**.

9. On the **Confirm installation selections** page, click **Install**.

10. On the **Installation progress** page, click **Close**.

Install Microsoft Deployment Toolkit 2012 Update 1

1. On **DC01**, go to **D:\MDT 2012 Update 1** and run the **MDT 2012 Update 1 Setup** (**MicrosoftDeploymentToolkit2012_x64.msi**).

2. On the **Welcome** page, click **Next**.

3. On the **End User License Agreement** page, select the **I accept the terms in the License Agreement** check box, and click **Next**.

4. On the **Custom Setup** page, accept the default settings and click **Next**.

5. On the **Customer Experience Improvement Program** page, accept the default settings and click **Next**.

6. On the **Ready to install Microsoft Deployment Toolkit 2012 Update 1** page, click **Install**.

7. After the installation is completed, click **Finish**.

CL01 Configuration

In these steps, I assume you have a virtual machine named CL01 with a default setup of Windows Server 8 Enterprise x64 edition installed to a single 127 GB partition and 2 GB of RAM.

Join the Machine to the Domain

1. On **CL01**, log in as a local **Administrator**.

2. Verify that the local computer name is **CL01**; otherwise, rename the machine **CL01**.

3. Join the machine to the **VIAMONSTRA** domain, and reboot when prompted.

4. On **DC01**, using **Active Directory Users and Computers**, move the **CL01** machine to the **Workstations** OU.

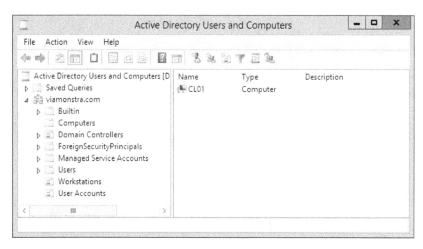

Active Directory Users and Computers, showing the CL01 computer account.

Install .NET Framework 3.5.1

1. On **CL01**, log in as **Administrator** in the **VIAMONSTRA** domain.

2. Mount the **Windows 8 Enterprise x64** ISO, and make sure it is the **D:** drive.

3. Start an elevated **command prompt** (run as administrator), and run the following command:

> **Dism.exe /Online /Enable-Feature /FeatureName:NetFX3 /Source:D:\sources\sxs**

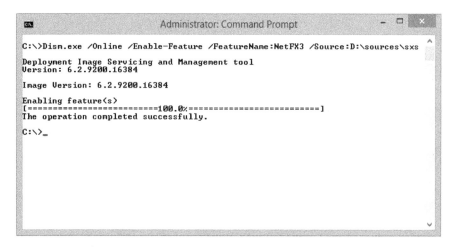

Enabling .NET Framework 3.5.1 via command line.

Index

Beyond the Book – Meet the Expert

If you liked his book, you will love to meet him in person.

Live Presentations

Andreas frequently speak at Microsoft conferences around the world, such as Microsoft TechEd. You also can find him at deployment tours and local events like Microsoft TechDays and various user group meetings. For current info on Andreas, check out his blog:

www.theexperienceblog.com

Live Instructor-Led Classes

Andreas conducts scheduled, instructor-led classes in Europe. For current dates and locations, see the following site:

www.addskills.se

Twitter

Andreas also tweet on the following alias:

@AndreasStenhall